WHY
SOCIALISM?

PSL PUBLICATIONS

SAN FRANCISCO

Why Socialism?

The contents were originally released in April 2008
as part of the *Socialism and Liberation* journal series.

Contributors

John Beacham, Ben Becker, Brian Becker, Jinette Cáceres,
Stefanie Fisher, Nathalie Hrizi, Crystal Kim,
Eugene Puryear, Silvio Rodrigues, Tahnee Stair

Technical Editors

Tina Landis, Keith Pavlik

PSL Publications

2969 Mission Street, Suite 200
San Francisco, CA 94110
(415) 821-6171
books@PSLweb.org

Why Socialism?

WHY SOCIALISM?

A goal and a program for victory

Why socialism?

THIS issue of *Socialism and Liberation* is devoted to the question: Why socialism? It is a question that takes on greater urgency with every passing day in the United States and around the world.

The articles in this journal take for granted that revolutionary change is needed. In that sense, the starting point for this journal is the exploitation of workers by bankers and corporate CEOs, the racist cops jailing and killing Black and Latino youth, the million families losing their homes to foreclosure. The starting point is that for millions of people in the United States—for the vast majority, in fact—the system is not working.

In an advanced capitalist country like the United States, the rule of the tiny minority is held up by a vast network of ideology, myths and propaganda to justify the unjustifiable. Despite the illusion of choice and variety illustrated by cable television offering 1,000 channels and internet media from every corner of the country, the message is remarkably uniform. The system of capitalism, despite its problems, is the best of all possible worlds. It is based on human nature. Humanity is corrupted, whether by greed or by "original sin," and so exploitation is natural.

But despite the mythology of the invincibility of capitalism, history has shown that capitalism cannot exist without people's resistance, protest and rebellion. For those who decide to stand up and say, "No more," the question, "Why socialism?" is not an academic question. For us, it is the modern version of the question: Which way forward? How can we change the world?

This issue of *Socialism and Liberation* is written for those who are ready to stand up and fight for a better world.

A point of clarity about the use of the world "socialism"—a word that is used repeatedly throughout this issue. By socialism, we mean the goal of our struggle: a world free from exploitation, racism, war and oppression, a classless society. It is the peaceful, planned society that Albert Einstein referred to in his 1949 essay titled "Why Socialism?"

By socialism, we also mean the efforts to construct that society, including the experiences of those revolutions that have uprooted capitalism and began constructing a society in the interests of the working class—both the successes and the failures. In this sense, we are not referring to an ideal but to a historical project.

Third, by socialism we mean the revolutionary struggle to achieve the goal of a classless society. As several of the articles here point out, there is a ruling class in the United States that benefits enormously from the capitalist system of exploitation, and it will not give up its power without a fight. So while in 1848, Karl Marx and Frederick Engels could not call their essay the "Socialist Manifesto" for fear of being mistaken for the non-revolutionary socialists that then dominated the working-class landscape, today we see in socialism its original fighting program.

"But don't you mean communism?" some might ask. The answer is yes. While Marx and Lenin distinguished communism as a classless society compared to socialism as a society where the state was withering away, we see the two as inextricably linked.

In other words, when we answer the question, "Why socialism?" we are answering why we need revolutionary change in the United States.

WHY NOW?

One might say, with good reason, that the need for socialism is nothing new. In some ways, the question has been answered since 1848, when Marx and Engels wrote the Communist Manifesto. But the question takes on new urgency today.

World capitalism is again experiencing the type of crisis that is built into its very nature. An economic crisis is already underway in the United States. The effects are being felt more and more across the country. They will be felt around the world.

Combined with the economic crisis is the inevitable outcome in the era of imperialism—war. The overthrow of the Soviet Union in 1991 opened an era of unparalleled conflict and war. The imperialist adventure in the Middle East has drawn the Pentagon into a situation that is both untenable and unavoidable.

War and depression: That is the volatile mix that offers only two outcomes: barbarism or revolution.

So posing the question "Why socialism?" today is an effort to intervene in this world struggle. It is not dispassionate or academic.

The Party for Socialism and Liberation was formed in 2004 on the premise of an upsurge and revival of the struggle for socialism—both in the United States and around the world. This issue of the PSL's journal is another step toward contributing to that upsurge.

BURNING QUESTIONS FOR TODAY

This journal takes up the question of "Why socialism?" from three points of view. The first section attempts to describe how socialism came about as a world view and as a program for action. It traces how socialism grew from a cry of the oppressed to a science of revolutionary change and how it provided, with accumulated experience in the living class struggle, a glimpse into what the future could be with the working class in command.

The second section is devoted to drawing lessons from the experience of the class struggle to show that socialism is a tested guide to victory. Marxism, which in modern times means incorporating the political and theoretical contributions of V.I. Lenin, is not the only political program for social change. Oppressed people have fought before having a program; they have also fought according to other programs, like anarchism or reformism. The articles in this section make the case that in the face of the much-repeated lie that "socialism has failed," both positive and negative experience show socialism as the only program that can win.

The final section aims to show that socialism is not a 19th-century philosophy—it provides the way forward to the burning issues facing poor and working people in the 21st-century United States. Racism, sexism, anti-LGBT oppression, unemployment, exploitation and environmental destruction—socialism provides the answer to the criminal legacy of capitalism.

THE COMMUNIST MANIFESTO TODAY

There is a hidden text running beneath this entire issue of *Socialism and Liberation*—that is Marx and Engel's Communist Manifesto. Although that pamphlet was written 160 years ago, using the language and references of a different period in the class struggle, it remains, to quote Eugene Puryear's article, "a living document in the hands of proletarian revolutionaries."

The Manifesto's clarion call, "Workers of the world unite, you have nothing to lose but your chains," was an urgent appeal for international working-class solidarity at a time when the European ruling classes were aiming to use the emerging working class as cannon fodder in their predatory wars of nationalist expansion. Workers were endlessly sent to war to kill other workers. Nationalist rivalries between capitalists left the appearance that workers could do nothing but hate and butcher each other. Uniting and rejecting bourgeois nationalism was not only the proletariat's answer to capitalist savagery. It also offered the only hope for a better world free from endless war.

In the wake of the 1917 Russian Revolution, the Communist International updated the slogan to the imperialist era, appealing to "workers and oppressed peoples." It was recognition that imperialist domination had generated multi-class movements in the oppressed world whose objective interests aligned them with the revolutionary proletarian movement.

Today, the peoples of the oppressed world are becoming more and more proletarian. When the multinational working class of the imperialist countries stretch out a hand of internationalist solidarity to the oppressed world, they are now more likely to meet the hand of a fellow worker than the peasant farmer or small owner of the past. The struggles against NAFTA and the Free Trade Area of the Americas offer real opportunities for this solidarity to emerge.

International working-class solidarity—that remains the foundation on which revolutionary socialism can grow and develop.

Why socialism? Because the future of humanity depends on it. □

THE DEVELOPMENT
OF SOCIALIST IDEAS

The first modern socialists

Utopian?
The means, not the goal

SINCE the advent of class antagonisms in human society, oppressed people and others angered by injustice have dreamed of a better world. In the face of poverty, disease, humiliation and exploitation, people have counterposed their hopes and aspirations for a life free of sorrows and worry, where the pain and suffering of daily life no longer exists.

In earlier centuries, those hopes frequently took form in a religious context. Since people are taught that suffering and exploitation are necessary features of human life—the ruling class always presents its exploitation as "natural" and "the way things are"—people look for refuge in an afterlife or a heaven.

"You will eat by and by," the old Joe Hill song parodies reactionary preachers, "in that glorious land in the sky. Work and pray, live on hay, you'll get pie in the sky when you die."

But not always were the dreams of a perfect world relegated to a far-off afterlife. Sometimes they inspired struggles for a better life in the here-and-now. For example, in the mid-19th century, a Chinese Christian visionary named Hong Xiuquan led a massive rebellion known as the Taiping Rebellion against the European-backed Qing dynasty.

Hong established a "Heavenly Kingdom." Private ownership of land was banned, foot binding of women was outlawed and restrictions on women were forbidden. Sexual relations between men and women were forbidden.

The Heavenly Kingdom was overthrown in 1861 by a combined Qing-French-British military campaign, but the Taiping Rebellion continued for another nine years.

All visions of a better world did not have religious roots, however.

9

During the Industrial Revolution in Europe during the 18th and 19th centuries, thinkers and philosophers grappled with the questions not just of what a better world would look like, but how to achieve it. As industrialization brought about the prospect of eradicating the problems associated with scarcity altogether, the quest for a better world took on a different outlook and character.

CONDITIONS GIVE RISE TO UTOPIAN SOCIALISM

At the root of this 18th- and 19th-century thinking was the contradiction between the promise of a society based on greater wealth and progress, on the one hand, and the realities of life for the vast majority of the working class on the other.

Frederick Engels describes the conditions of the industrial working class in Britain, for example, as "social murder," because the ruling forces of society intentionally placed workers in a position where premature and unnatural deaths were inevitable.[1]

The conditions of the British working class were much like those for workers in other industrializing countries. Engels was one of many to document how workers—even young children—worked 14 hours a day in dangerous factories and mines, in order to meet the demands of burgeoning capitalist production. Major injuries and deaths resulting from dangerous working conditions were common. Hundreds of children died of neglect as mothers and fathers locked their children in the house and left home to earn meager wages. The annual rate of death in England was 22.2 for every 1,000 persons.[2] (By comparison, the 2007 mortality rate in the United States was 8.26 per 1,000 persons.)

Mass migration to urban areas in search of work led to oppressive living conditions. As many as a dozen workers shared a single room. Without proper public services in place, the streets were filled with garbage and excrement. Overcrowding and poor ventilation, along with rampant pollution from factories, created severe respiratory problems for many workers. Clean water was largely inaccessible. Overcrowding resulted in several epidemics of typhus, causing tens of thousands of deaths.

On top of all this, most workers suffered from insufficient clothing and diet. Conditions were particularly difficult for immigrant workers, who had to endure discrimination in addition to the widespread sufferings of the working class.

The cruel realities of the industrial working class exposed the exploitative nature of capitalism. At the same time, rapid industrialization and socialized production brought with it the reality that societies could be established on the basis of abundance rather than scarcity.

This reality led to the idea of early socialist intellectuals that human society could and should be transformed into a truly democratic world—a socialist world—where there would be no exploitation of one class by another, and the needs of all people would be met.

'EVOLVING FROM THE BRAIN'

Karl Marx and Frederick Engels called these early socialist thinkers "utopian socialists"—a reference to the term popularized by a 16th-century writer Sir Thomas More about a perfect society that could never really exist. Marx and Engels called the thinkers utopian not because of their ultimate aim but because of their proposed methodology to achieve that aim.

While utopian socialists had visions of societies that would ultimately influence the works of Marx and Engels, their visions did not include a scientific evaluation of the reality of the class struggle and how a better world could be achieved out of those material conditions. For this reason, in his classic exposition "Socialism: Utopian and Scientific," Engels writes that utopian socialism "attempted to evolve out of the human brain."[3]

For example, Henri de Saint-Simon (1770-1825), believed that 18th-century French society could be transformed into a rational and harmonious society led by philosophers and scientists in the interests of the greater good for society. He pointed out the class struggle, although he portrayed it as the struggle between those who work and those who are "idle."

Charles Fourier (1772-1837), Saint-Simon's contemporary, envisioned cooperative communities called "phalanxes" in which disparities in wealth would still exist but less desirable work would receive higher pay. He subjected bourgeois society to the most scathing criticism, pointing to how exploitation lay at the core of "civilization."

Fourier was also one of the early proponents of women's liberation. Engels notes that Fourier "was the first to declare that in any given society the degree of women's emancipation is the natural measure of the general emancipation."[4]

Both of these thinkers set about to make their ideal worlds a reality—by appealing to the good nature of France's liberal bourgeoisie. Saint-Simon initially sought to win over scientists and philosophers to take up his social causes. He sought out bankers and "enlightened" bourgeoisie. Many of his followers ended up forming quasi-religious societies.[5] Likewise, Fourier hoped to find wealthy and educated capitalists to fund his social projects. One banker, Jacques Lafitte, politely turned down Fourier's pleas for assistance, while acknowledging he was "flattered by what [Fourier] said of the influence which his name would have in France."[6]

UTOPIA IN PRACTICE: NEW LANARK

While both Saint-Simon and Fourier had followers who at various times in the 19th century attempted to implement this or that element of social reform, Robert Owen (1771-1858) set out to put his ideas into practice.

Owen, a wealthy Welshman, was perhaps the best-known utopian socialist. Along with his business partners, Owen bought the cotton mills of New Lanark, Scotland in 1800, when he was 29. He strongly believed that people were a product of their environment, and strove to improve the productivity of New Lanark through prioritizing the welfare of the people rather than profits.

Owens was determined to improve working conditions. Engels noted that the working day in New Lanark was 10 1/2 hours, as compared to 13 or 14 hours a day at competing mills. When New Lanark workers were out of work, they continued to receive their full wages.

Due to the value placed upon the well-being and integrity of the working class, the workers of New Lanark were extremely productive. Its population of 2,500 produced as much as a population of 600,000 would have produced 50 years earlier. Further, drunkenness, police, magistrates, lawsuits, poor laws and charity were unknown in the community.[7]

Despite the vast social and commercial successes of New Lanark, Engels notes that Owen was not content: "The existence which he secured for his workers was, in his eyes, still far from being worthy of human beings. 'The people were slaves at my mercy.'"[8]

Owen referred to the fact that while the condition of workers in New Lanark were far superior to those of workers elsewhere, they were still subordinate to the rules of capital. At the end of the day, it was the investors of the New Lanark mills who pocketed the profit.

Owen's solution to this dilemma was to build a society based on collective work and ownership—a kind of communism. He believed that the ruling class would be won over by the sheer rationality of communism and would cooperate in its establishment. After all, as a businessman and philanthropist who improved the lives of thousands in New Lanark, Owen was considered a hero. The ruling class praised his project when it was seen as a charitable experiment—and he made money at the same time.

Yet when Owen began advocating his ideas of establishing communism on a wider scale and abolishing private property, he became an outcast from public life. He soon began to organize socialist communities in the United States, including the most well-known one in New Harmony, Indiana.

DOOMED TO FAILURE

Owen's proposal for building communism could not succeed because Owen, like the other utopian socialists, did not take into consideration the irreconcilable class contradictions that govern capitalist society. As Engels explained, utopian socialism "criticized the existing capitalistic mode of production and its consequences. But it could not explain them, and, therefore, could not get the mastery of them."[9]

Owen was further disgraced when his communitarian project in New Harmony, Indiana, failed, partially due to the fact that his business partner ran off with all the profits.

The rule of the capitalist class is dependent upon the complete irrationality of the capitalist economic system. The utopian socialists did not understand the dynamics of capitalism, namely that the class interests of the ruling class and the working class are in direct opposition to each other. They did not understand the impossibility of building alternative social orders within the framework of world capitalism or the need to uproot capitalist exploitation entirely.

Marx and Engels, despite their efforts to differentiate their scientific socialism from the utopian socialism of Saint-Simon, Fourier and Owen, did not subject them to the same fierce criticism that they did to other later political opponents within the working-class movement. On the contrary, they gave the utopians credit for seeing the outlines of a new society—before the social agent to make those dreams a reality was able to take center stage.

> *Socialism and communism are not utopian goals. They are perfectly rational and humane models for society.*

In fact, the main limitation of the utopians was the fact that they were trying to develop a socialist vision before the class that would be able to fulfill it was fully formed. The modern wage working class— the proletariat—only emerged as a political force with the Chartist movement in England in the 1830s and in the European revolutions of 1848.

The same cannot be said of the modern-day "communes" and "intentional communities." With the class struggle raging in the 21st century, with the examples of working-class power and even efforts to build socialism, these efforts sometime share the same form as the utopian socialists of the 19th century, but none of the revolutionary content. They are escapist fantasies for petty-bourgeois elements who are trying to escape from the very class struggle that can lead to a new society.

MAKING DREAMS A REALITY

Socialism and communism are not utopian goals. They are perfectly rational and humane models for society. For the first time in history, we are able to produce enough goods and services to meet the needs of all people—and in a way that will not destroy the environment in the process. On the contrary, it is capitalism—a system that hoards the fruits of the labor of poor and working people for profit—that is completely irrational.

Realizing the dreams and aspirations of oppressed and exploited people will take more than the visions of the most advanced and enlightened thinkers, however. It will take the application of scientific

methods to understand the motor force of history—the class struggle—
and to unlock the tremendous social power of the working class. □

Endnotes

1. The Conditions of the Working Class in England, p. 108-9.
2. Ibid., p. 118.
3. F. Engels, "Socialism: Utopian and Scientific," in Karl Marx and Frederick Engels Selected Works, Vol. 3, Progress Publishers, 1970, p. 119.
4. Ibid, p. 122.
5. Booth, Arthur John, "Saint-Simon and Saint-Simonism," Longmans, Green, Reader and Dyer, 1871, p. 23-24, 40.
6. Pellarin, Charles, "The Life of Charles Fourier," W.H. Graham, 1848, p. 73. See also p. 56, pp. 63f.
7. Engels, p. 123.
8. Engels, p.124.
9. Engels, p.133

Karl Marx

The Communist Manifesto

A working-class guide to changing the world

THE Communist Manifesto stands among the most well-read books of all time. One hundred sixty years after it was first published, it has been reprinted hundreds of times in most of the world's languages. It has been praised, slandered, banned and distorted.

Certainly more than any other political pamphlet, the Communist Manifesto has stood the test of time. It is studied in schools, colleges, workplaces, activist study groups and underground discussion groups all over the world.

The reason that the Communist Manifesto remains such an inspiration for revolutionary change is that it is not just the musings of social reformers, philosophers or political wannabes. It is a working class guide for changing the world.

WRITTEN IN THE HEAT OF BATTLE

Karl Marx and Frederick Engels wrote the Manifesto in 1848 when they were 29 and 27 years old, respectively. All of Europe was in turmoil. In France, there was growing dissatisfaction with the "bourgeois king" Louis Philippe. National uprisings against the Austro-Hungarian empire were just under the surface. Opposition to the feudal monarchs ruling the German and Italian states was mounting along with growing demands for national unification.

Much of this discontent came from petty-bourgeois shopkeepers and intellectuals. In France, this class had been instrumental in the 1789 bourgeois revolution but had been sidelined under Louis Philippe. In the rest of continental Europe, they were still politically disenfranchised. These forces were mainly interested in becoming the new ruling class.

Skilled artisans also felt the bite of the newly emerging capitalist social system. Loss of their guilds forced many of them into traveling communities of workers that moved anywhere to find work. The ranks of the former artisans, now workers, spawned many radical activists who believed in the struggle for, as Engels said, "total social change."

The bourgeoisie was relatively unconcerned with addressing the problems of the new working classes. Workers were forced to labor 13 to 15 hours a day and live in run-down and disease-ridden slums. Their numbers were constantly increasing. They had been pauperized by the economic changes of capitalism around them.

The emergence of the modern working class as a political force was the main element that separated the political climate in the late 1840s from the revolutionary ferments of earlier years.

From the new working class, secretive revolutionary organizations sprung up across Europe. Some were inspired by earlier socialists like Saint-Simon or Fourier. Others were inspired by internationalists like Philippe Buonarroti and Gracchus Babeuf, leaders of the extreme left wing of the French Revolution. Militants like Louis Auguste Blanqui tried to set up insurrectionary groups in France.

One such group, the League of the Just, had participated with Blanqui's supporters in an uprising in Paris in 1839.[1] It was this group, renamed in 1847 as the Communist League, that commissioned the young radicals Marx and Engels in December 1847 to draft a program for the anticipated uprisings. In February 1848, the Communist Manifesto appeared as the fighting program of the Communist League.

The Manifesto appeared on the streets of Paris shortly before the February 1848 uprising in that city. That uprising spread with revolutionary fervor across Europe. This revolutionary wave gave the Manifesto an audience among revolutionary activists, raising Marx's profile in the working-class movement.

THE SCIENCE OF SOCIAL CHANGE

What separated the Communist Manifesto from the dozens of programs and manifestos issued by other revolutionary groups of the day? Why are all those other programs forgotten today but the Manifesto is still widely read? What is it that has given this small pamphlet the ability to captivate Alabama sharecroppers, Russian revolutionaries and Chinese peasants alike?

Marx and Engels incorporated the most advanced political, economic and philosophical thought of the time into scientific socialism: determining the laws by which society changed and then applying those laws to bring about socialism and, in due course, a communist society.

They applied the dialectical method of the German philosopher Georg Hegel to the materialism of the most advanced scientific thinkers. In this way, they were able to identify class struggle as the motive force of history. Based on an economic analysis of capitalist society and the historical development of society's productive forces, they identified the working class as the only "really revolutionary class," the class that had the potential not only to liberate itself but all of humanity.

Starting with their often-quoted phrase, "The history of all hitherto existing society is the history of class struggle," the two young revolutionaries sketched in a popular way the history of class struggle from its beginning until 1848. In this way, they were able to put the individual struggles of workers in this city or that country into the overall framework of the struggle of exploited against exploiters. It is that context that allows the Manifesto to speak to revolutionaries around the world struggling against capitalism.

ROOTED IN WORKING-CLASS ORGANIZATION

The historic significance of the Communist Manifesto is not only due to the brilliance of the ideas that Marx and Engels elaborated. They themselves acknowledged that most of the essential ideas in the Manifesto had already been elaborated—although not in a unified way.

The importance of the Manifesto can hardly be overstated. It is not just a pamphlet, but the program of a revolutionary workers' organization in the ongoing struggle against capitialism. The defeat of the 1848 revolutions led to major reprisals against revolutionaries. The Communist League was disbanded amid the anti-communist trials in Cologne in 1852.[2] Undeterred, Marx and Engels continued toward the task outlined in the Manifesto, the "organization of the proletarians into a class and consequently into a political party."

Marx's position in the International Workers' Association (the First International) kept the program of the Manifesto in the minds of working-class revolutionaries, even though the specific demands had changed to meet the new political circumstances. This in turn led to the founding of mass socialist parties in Germany and France, expanding the reach of the Manifesto as the foundational document for many who considered themselves socialists and communists into the first half of the 20th century.

> *It is the reality of the class struggle that continues to make the Communist Manifesto a living document in the hands of proletarian revolutionaries.*

The triumph of the 1917 Russian Revolution opened the era of proletarian revolution. For the first time, the document that had accompanied the working class sectors of the 1848 revolutions showed itself as a guide to victory in the hands of the Bolshevik Party led by V.I. Lenin. In addition to the tremendous inspiration that the October Revolution offered for workers and oppressed people around the world, the new Soviet state was able to print, translate and distribute innumerable copies of the Manifesto to areas where it once had to be printed secretly or in limited press runs.

The text of the Manifesto is more or less unchanged since 1848. Already in 1872, Marx and Engels referred to the Manifesto as a "historical document, which we no longer have any right to alter."

It is the reality of the class struggle that continues to make the Communist Manifesto a living document in the hands of proletarian revolutionaries. For example, the death of "laissez-faire" free market capitalism required the Communist International under Lenin's political influence to update the Manifesto's immortal slogan "Workers of the world, unite!" to "Workers and oppressed people of the world, unite!" Imperialism had extended the tentacles of monopoly capital to every corner of the world, meaning that the overthrow of capitalist social relations would come from revolutionary workers and the legions of nationally oppressed people around the world whose development had been brutally strangled by the machinations of trusts and combines.

Now more than ever, with the speed at which capital is being accumulated in fewer and fewer hands, as the already-socialized division of labor is becoming increasingly international, the observations of Marx and Engels provide a way forward. The Manifesto is not just a critique of capitalism or a manual for revolutionary strategy. It is a compelling argument anticipating that the modern working class would not be simply a victim of oppression but act as the new vanguard that would reconstruct society. This achievement in communist propaganda, in turn, became a material factor accelerating the formation of communist and socialist organizations wherever the workers awakened to political life.

To this day, the Manifesto inspires revolutionaries the world over to struggle for the overthrow of the rule of capital. From Venezuela and Colombia and across Latin America, with the red banner still raised high by revolutionary Cuba, from the Philippines to Palestine, from the belly of the beast of U.S. imperialism, the closing words of the Communist Manifesto still ring clear:

"Let the ruling classes tremble at a Communistic revolution. The proletarians have nothing to lose but their chains. They have a world to win." □

Endnotes

1. Struik, Dirk, "The Birth of the Communist Manifesto," International Publishers, 1971, p. 52.
2. Cf. Engels, Frederick, "On the History of the Communist League" (1885) in Marx and Engels Selected Works vol. 3, Progress Publishers, 1970, p. 173.

The 'dictatorship of the proletariat'

How can the working class defend its revolution?

WORKERS around the world have instinctively understood the need for a union. In the fight against the bosses—whether it is for pay and benefits, better working conditions or to defend the gains they have already won—individual workers standing alone lose, while workers uniting together can win.

While today some jobs come with health care benefits, this was not always the case. Health care benefits were won through militant workers' struggles by unions against the capitalist bosses. As soon as gains are won by the workers, however, the capitalist boss inevitably tries to reduce or eliminate these advances to maximize profit.

Through unions, the working class organizes to defend gains won by organizing, by setting up picket lines, by striking and other actions.

Throughout the 20th century, workers waged much larger struggles—not just to protect themselves from the exploitation of their employers, but to uproot their exploiters once and for all. The socialist revolutions in Russia, China, Korea, Albania, Yugoslavia, Vietnam, Cuba and others all set out with this aim. Each time, the question has been posed: How will the working class—the new ruling class—organize to protect itself from imperialist attack and counterrevolution?

Karl Marx and Frederick Engels anticipated the question as early as 1848 in the Communist Manifesto. "We have seen," they wrote, "that the first step in the revolution by the working class is to raise the proletariat to the position of ruling class, to win the battle of democracy." For the first time, the ruling class will consist of the vast majority of society instead of a tiny few.

"The proletariat will use its political supremacy to wrest, by degrees, all capital from the bourgeoisie, to centralize all instruments of production in the hands of the State, i.e. of the proletariat

23

organized as the ruling class; and to increase the total of productive forces as rapidly as possible," they continued.

The working class would need to organize as the ruling class. Long before workers had ever successfully held power, Marx and Engels could see the need for organizing politically—with the tools of state power—against the power and wealth of the bourgeoisie.

As much as the working class would like it not to be the case, the capitalist class and the legacy of class division remain following the seizure of power. All kinds of inequality in income and personal property holdings, as well as racism and sexism, do not disappear on their own immediately after a workers' revolution. The ideological influence of the bourgeoisie encompasses more than the class of exploiters. The preeminence of bourgeois ideology, reinforced by material stratification inside society, in turn provides a base for counterrevolution following a socialist revolution.

> The concept of the 'dictatorship of the proletariat' became a central feature of revolutionary socialism.

The experience of the Soviet Union shows that the possibility of capitalist restoration remains long after a revolutionary triumph.

Marx and Engels were writing on the eve of the 1848 revolutions. The working class was in the streets, and Marx and Engels were among the few to see in this class the potential to "organize as the ruling class." In summing up the experiences of the 1848 uprisings in France, Marx noted in his essay "Class Struggles in France, 1848-1850" that "there appeared the bold slogan of revolutionary struggle: Overthrow of the bourgeoisie! Dictatorship of the working class!"

The concept of the "dictatorship of the proletariat" became a central feature of revolutionary socialism. It also became one of the most misunderstood concepts, used by enemies of Marxism to prove that communism was in essence dictatorial and anti-democratic.

ALL POWER TO THE WORKERS!

On Jan. 1, 1852, one of Marx's close colleagues in the United States, Joseph Weydemeyer, published an article titled "The Dictatorship of the Proletariat" in a German-language newspaper. Marx responded in a famous letter dated March 5, 1852:

Long before me, bourgeois historians had described the historical development of this class struggle and bourgeois economists, the economic anatomy of the classes. What I did that was new was to prove: 1) That the existence of classes is only bound up with particular historical phases in the development of production, 2) that the class struggle necessarily leads to the dictatorship of the proletariat, 3) that this dictatorship itself only constitutes the transition to the abolition of all classes and to a classless society.

Two points immediately emerge. First, Marx was not writing about a particular form of government; rather, he referred to dictatorship in the sense of exclusive class power. The interests of the working class were diametrically opposed to those of the capitalist class, and a state could serve only one class. The dictatorship of the proletariat was a precise class phrase that expressed a slogan popularized by the U.S. Black Panther Party in the late 1960s: "All power to the people!"

Second, the exclusive power in the hands of the working class was seen as a step toward the abolition of class exploitation overall.

THE PARIS COMMUNE

"Of late, the Social-Democratic philistine has once more been filled with wholesome terror at the words: Dictatorship of the Proletariat. Well and good, do you want to know what this dictatorship looks like? Look at the Paris Commune. That was the Dictatorship of the Proletariat."

Those were Engels' words in his 1891 introduction to Marx's work "The Civil War in France."

Marx wrote more about the dictatorship of the proletariat following the 1871 Paris Commune. The Commune was the first example of a working-class government—a model for a socialist state—even though the workers only held power for two months before being drowned in blood. The experience of the Commune proved the necessity of the dictatorship of the proletariat.

The Paris Commune was formed after workers seized power in Paris following the French defeat in the Franco-Prussian war. Originally set up to defend the capital against a Prussian invasion, the Commune soon had to face both French and Prussian troops.

How did the workers organize themselves against the combined threat of military invasion and bourgeois counterrevolution? The Commune abolished the standing army and police and armed the workers. Officials were elected by universal suffrage and could be immediately recalled. Officials were elected regardless of nationality and were paid a worker's wage.

The Commune was not a talk shop. Unlike "democratic" congresses and parliaments, its members were responsible for carrying out the laws they passed.

In addition, rents were reduced, interest on debts was abolished and educational institutions were opened up, among many social measures that benefited the working class.

While recognizing the Paris Commune as the first genuine workers' government, Marx also analyzed the reason for its downfall: its failure to take relentless action against the defeated ruling class that had fled to Versailles. The Commune's hesitation and moderation allowed the French capitalists to regroup before retaking Paris amid the vicious slaughter of tens of thousands of French workers.

TOWARD A CLASSLESS SOCIETY

The experience of the Paris Commune proved decisive as Marx and Engels attempted to orient the German socialist movement in a revolutionary direction. They used many of the lessons in the debates surrounding the program of the German Socialist Workers Party in 1875—the so-called "Gotha Program," named after the town where the socialist delegates met.

In "Critique of the Gotha Program," Marx further explained the necessity of the establishment of a dictatorship of the proletariat through revolutionary struggle. Socialism could not be achieved through universal suffrage or winning reforms from the capitalist state.

Since the Gotha Program aimed to set out the goals of German socialists, Marx outlined the main features of communism—classless society. Under communism, exploitation would not exist and society's wealth would be so great that the general principle of "from each according to their ability, to each according to their need" could be realized.

Marx also outlined socialism as a "lower stage" of communism, where private exploitation would be abolished but certain inequalities would still exist due to the lack of productive forces or remaining "birth marks of the old society." During this period, wealth would be allocated according to the workers' contributions to society as opposed to their needs.

But most importantly, Marx laid out the need for an intermediate stage. "Between capitalist and communist society lies the period of the revolutionary transformation of the one into the other. Corresponding to this is also a political transition period in which the state can be nothing but the revolutionary dictatorship of the proletariat."

Engels, in a follow-up letter to Socialist leader August Bebel, is more blunt: "The state is only a transitional institution which is used in the struggle, in the revolution, to hold down one's adversaries by force."

V.I. Lenin, the leader of the Russian Revolution, provided further analysis of the dictatorship of the proletariat in his 1917 pamphlet "State and Revolution." He explained that the significance of Marx's explanation of the dictatorship of the proletariat was that he showed it was "something which develops out of capitalism" and that it is not "scholastically invented."

THE EXPERIENCE OF THE SOCIALIST REVOLUTIONS

The experience of the Russian Revolution and later revolutions in Cuba, Korea, Vietnam, China and elsewhere showed that the dictatorship of the proletariat is a necessary element to the defense, survival and growth of working-class rule. Unlike the original projections of the first socialist thinkers, workers overthrew their capitalist exploiters first not in the most developed countries but in the most oppressed and underdeveloped societies.

The transition to socialism and the envisioned "withering away of the state"—the diminished need for the suppression of counter-revolution—was a much more difficult task. In each case, the workers' state served to stave off imperialist intervention and counter-revolution while desperately attempting to develop the productive forces of society.

The states established by the new revolutionary governments acted like unions, defending the workers in a world where the bosses were the imperialist giants, armed to the teeth with nuclear weapons and other weapons of mass destruction.

Class struggle did not end after the victory of the socialist revolutions. In fact, it became even more intense. That was the reason that the early Bolsheviks looked with such hope toward victorious revolutions in the imperialist countries.

Just as bosses attempt to take back gains won by the workers through the union struggles, the capitalists attempt to return to power after a working-class revolution has made the working class the ruling class of society.

In order to organize itself effectively, the new workers' state must destroy the old capitalist state that was used to repress the working class—its army, police, prisons and courts—and replace them with an entirely new socialist state to organize for the defense of the revolution. The new state is based on institutions and laws that serve the interests of the working class.

To write the next chapter in the development of the revolutionary socialist theory on the transition to communism will require new experiences. The greatest contribution would be a socialist revolution in the United States, where the productive forces are great enough to lay the foundation for liberating the world's working class. □

The goal of socialism

Peace and equality amid plenty

WHAT will socialist society look like?

The earliest pioneers of scientific socialism—Karl Marx and Frederick Engels—did not philosophize about what socialism and communism would look like in detail. Nor did they discuss how long it would take to transform society from capitalism to socialism.

In "The German Ideology," one of his early writings from 1845, Marx wrote the famous lines: "In communist society, where nobody has one exclusive sphere of activity but each can become accomplished in any branch he wishes, society regulates the general production and thus makes it possible for me to do one thing today and another tomorrow, to hunt in the morning, fish in the afternoon, rear cattle in the evening, criticize [philosophize] after dinner, just as I have a mind, without ever becoming hunter, fisherman, herdsman or critic."

No one, Marx included, took this as a literal forecast of what communism would look like. It was seen rather as a way of illustrating the division of labor that future communist societies would inherit from the preceding class society.

Instead, Marx and Engels devoted much of their work to creating an outline of economic development based on a thorough analysis of capitalism. Their goal was to determine what a new society could look like, as opposed to earlier socialists who tried to dictate what society should look like.

Marxism, as scientific socialism is known today, begins with the struggle between antagonistic classes in society. The class struggle has taken different forms throughout history, from the struggle between slaves and masters in ancient Egypt and Rome to the struggle of serfs against landlords in feudal Europe.

By the time Marx and Engels were writing, the classes had become even more widely separated. The overwhelming majority of working people were forced to labor daily in order to meet their basic needs, while a tiny minority reaped more and more profit from the exploited classes. The working class, which was growing in size and social weight, represented those of the exploited classes that had to sell their labor power on a daily basis in order to survive. This condition continues today.

In the working class, Marx saw not only the force that could overthrow capitalist exploitation, but also the foundation for a classless society without exploitation—communism. "If the proletariat during its contest with the bourgeoisie is compelled, by the force of circumstances, to organize itself as a class," Marx and Engels wrote in the Communist Manifesto, "if by means of a revolution it makes itself the ruling class and, as such, sweeps away by force the old conditions of production, then it will, along with these conditions, have swept away the conditions for the existence of class antagonisms and of classes generally."

TRANSITION TO COMMUNISM

At the heart of the Marxist conception of the socialist revolution is a dialectical understanding of social change: History evolves according to laws of motion governed by the conflict of opposing forces, with the outcome depending on what has come before. In particular, socialist and communist society can come about not by will or by design alone, but as the result of overcoming capitalist society through revolutionary struggle.

"What we have to deal with here is a communist society, not as it has developed on its own foundations, but, on the contrary, just as it emerges from capitalist society," Marx wrote in the 1872 "Critique of the Gotha Program." The new society is "thus in every respect, economically, morally and intellectually, still stamped with the birthmarks of the old society from whose womb it emerges."

It was in the "Critique of the Gotha Program" that Marx was most specific about what he could discern about the future socialist and communist society.

The first task, he wrote, was to smash the capitalist class' state apparatus—the dictatorship of the bourgeoisie—and replace it with the dictatorship of the proletariat. The working class would need a period to repress the efforts of the former ruling class to regain political power.

What was unique about the workers' state was that it sows the seeds for its own elimination or transformation from a state to a non-state. As the state representing the interests of the vast majority, for the first time in history, the workers' state would gradually reduce the mechanism for class repression—first, by eliminating exploitation that gave rise to the need for a state. This first step, though, requires the creation of generalized equality through the elimination of material scarcity. Under the new socialist order, the growth of the means of production, to the point where society's abundance eliminates the individual struggle for existence, allows for the gradual withering away of the state. It is a process rooted in material advances, not a decree or edict, that abolishes the state.

Once the purely defensive needs of the workers' state are completed, the real tasks of socialist construction can begin. During this first phase of communist society—Lenin notes in "State and Revolution" that this phase is generally known as socialism—the main task will be the enhancement of the productive forces and the overcoming of the "birthmarks of the old society."

SOCIALISM: 'TO EACH ACCORDING TO THEIR WORK'

The lower phase of communism, Marx projected, would be based on the slogan, "From each according to their ability, to each according to their work." He described this as follows: "The individual producer receives back from society—after the deductions have been made—exactly what he gives to it. ... The same amount of labor which is given to society in one form is received back in another."

This is a huge step forward from life under capitalism. Under capitalism, workers receive less in the form of wages than the full amount of their labor. The owning class appropriates a share of the value produced by the laborer in the form of private profit.

Nevertheless, Marx pointed out that this lower phase of communism is still an unequal economic arrangement—that it is still based on the "bourgeois right" of formal equality, or political-economic equality among unequal people. For example, this formal "equal right" enforces inequality of people with different needs. It does not take into account the number of children in a workers' family, for example, or the physical or mental capacity of the worker. There are further inequalities between skilled and unskilled workers and mental and physical labor.

"With an equal performance of labor," Marx noted, "and hence an equal share in the social consumption fund, one will in fact receive more than another, one will be richer than another, and so on."

Russian revolutionary leader V.I. Lenin elaborated on this theme in "State and Revolution:" "Of course, bourgeois right in regard to the distribution of articles of consumption inevitably presupposes the existence of the bourgeois state, for right is nothing without an apparatus capable of enforcing the observance of the standards of right. It follows that under communism there remains for a time not only bourgeois right, but even the bourgeois state—without the bourgeoisie!"

The reality of inequality also endures because individuals in bourgeois society are profoundly stratified at the time of the revolution. For example, millions of people in the United States own large homes—sometimes more than one—and have large savings and assets. An even larger number have next to nothing.

Unless the workers' state was to immediately expropriate the assets of what is known as the "upper middle class"—an act that would cause immense social turmoil following the revolution—this facet of inequality will remain for some time. Equal payment for labor performed, while a huge step forward, does not eradicate the vast inequality that is derived from the bourgeois society.

THE HIGHER STAGE OF COMMUNISM

A bourgeois state without the bourgeoisie—this is the distinctive feature under socialism as opposed to the higher stage of communism. This state under socialism, however, has a feature unheard of under capitalism. In the words of Frederick Engels in the 1878 pamphlet "Anti-Dühring:" "It withers away."

Lenin spent a significant portion of "State and Revolution" clarifying the Marxist conception of the withering away of the state. In particular, he pointed out against the reformists that the capitalist state does not wither away—the capitalist state must be uprooted in the course of workers' revolution.

But under socialism—after the revolution—the need for the state as a repressive apparatus gradually changes to an administrative organ for running society. Against "bourgeois right," the new society will be able to develop the productive forces to such an extent that the inequalities in society can be overcome.

"The economic basis for the complete withering away of the state," Lenin wrote, "is such a high level of development of communism at which the antithesis between mental and physical labor disappears, at which there consequently disappears one of the principal sources of modern social inequality—a source, moreover, which cannot on any account be removed immediately by the mere conversion of the means of production into public property, by the mere expropriation of the capitalists. ...

"The state will be able to wither away completely when society adopts the rule: 'From each according to their ability, to each according to their needs.'"

Lenin wrote those words in 1917, on the eve of the first socialist revolution the world had yet seen, in the former Russian empire. He, with Marx and Engels, had only the experience of the two months of the Paris Commune on which to base their analyses.

He acknowledged as much when he noted that "we are entitled to speak only of the inevitable withering away of the state ... leaving the question of the time required for, or the concrete forms of, the withering away quite open, because there is no material for answering these questions."

EXPERIENCES IN SOCIALIST CONSTRUCTION

Thanks in great part to the practical experience of Lenin in making revolution, 21st-century socialists have a wealth of experience on which to base further conclusions. Marxists have been able to use accumulated theory and practice in order to lead revolutions in Russia, China, Korea, Yugoslavia, Cuba and many other countries.

While there have been vast differences in the experiences of those socialist revolutions, they share one common feature: The socialist revolutions of the 20th century took place in countries where the level of productive forces was very low compared to the imperialist countries. Every successful revolution faced the primary task of developing their economies—while under constant military threat by world imperialism.

For that reason, Lenin described the challenges of building communism in 1920 in very practical terms: "Communism is Soviet power plus the electrification of the whole country." There was no hope in building socialism if the economy remained underdeveloped.

Because of the combined challenges of developing the productive forces under the gun of world imperialism, no socialist revolution has yet reached a stage where the "withering away of the state" could be imagined. Imperialism has seized on any weakness in the revolutionary states in order to foment counterrevolution.

Nevertheless, the working classes in the countries that have set out to build socialism have made tremendous gains. Russia's working class in 1917 was 4 percent of the population. Within 50 years, it was the second-most powerful economy in the world.

China had never been able to feed its entire population prior to the revolution. Millions died during famines in China prior to 1949. Yet after the 1949 revolution, for the first time the economy was able to feed the largest population in the world.

Socialist production has allowed Cuba to develop its economy in the interests of working people.

PHOTO: BILL HACKWELL

Despite immense pressure from imperialism, Cuba has been able to achieve tremendous gains—despite the collapse of the Soviet Union in 1991. Cuban workers enjoy among the highest living standards of any of their counterparts in Latin America or much of the oppressed world.

The continued military and economic dominance by world imperialism—first and foremost by U.S. imperialism—has made the transition to socialism that Marx and Lenin described so far impossible. The workers' states have needed to devote a considerable part of their social development toward the strengthening of the proletarian dictatorship—the army and police—in order to defend against invasion or counterrevolution.

Taking that next step will require a society based on the dictatorship of the proletariat in the United States. Toppling the world's dominant capitalist power would not only lift a tremendous burden from the workers around the world who are trying to engage in socialist construction. It would put at the disposal of the world working class the tremendous wealth produced by the U.S. working class. All the social wealth extracted from the oppressed world by U.S. corporations and mines could be used to reverse the effects of centuries of colonial and imperialist exploitation.

A revolution in the United States would undercut the economic basis for divisions among the working class that promote racism, sexism and homophobia.

Socialism is a system of peace, justice and equality. The road to socialism begins with revolution in the United States. □

HISTORICAL EXPERIENCE AND SOCIALIST REVOLUTION

Rebellion and the need for organization

"**T**HE history of all hitherto existing society is the history of class struggles." In one sentence, Karl Marx and Frederick Engels captured the essential driving force of class society.

Engels later amended the original formulation to account for the discovery of pre-class societies based on communal rather than private property, where class struggle was absent. The fundamental truth about class society, however, remains true.

In the recollection of human conflict, historical accounts often focus on the roles played by leaders. While leadership is certainly essential in determining the direction that the struggle takes, no leader, no matter how charismatic or eloquent, can stir the masses into struggle when they find themselves in relative comfort and peace.

It is the contradictions of class society that inevitably propel the masses into action. In all class societies, the wealth and privilege of the owning class rests on the exploitation of the toiling masses. This lays the basis for ever-present conflict, which from time to time erupts from a simmer to a boil as the burden on the shoulders of the oppressed becomes intolerable.

INDIVIDUAL RESISTANCE

The struggle against slavery in the United States is often summed up in the events of the Civil War, with white abolitionists taking center stage. However, the history of U.S. slavery is rich in examples of resistance where the enslaved Africans themselves were the protagonists.

Black slaves in the pre-Civil War South frequently poisoned their masters and their families, leading to a whole system of special laws prohibiting this form of resistance. In 1751, South Carolina decreed the death penalty for any Black found guilty of poisoning a white. The preamble of a similar law passed in 1770 in Georgia explained its motivation: "Whereas, the detestable crime of poisoning hath frequently been committed by slaves ..."

Arson was even more common, to the point it affected the policy of insurance companies. An American Fire Insurance Company of Philadelphia official, in response to a request in 1820, explained that the company "declined making insurance in any of the slave states." Savannah was frequently hit by arson, usually blamed on slaves. Residents of Charleston, South Carolina, organized a committee in the 1790s to ensure the use of brick or stone rather than wood in housing construction.[1]

REBELLION

The frequency and prevalence of such incidents show that the will to struggle was widespread among the slaves. Yet these acts amounted to disconnected resistance on the part of individuals or, at most, very small groups acting in an atomized manner. It was when their shared will to struggle manifested itself as collective resistance that their power as a class was felt.

During research for his seminal "American Negro Slave Revolts," Herbert Aptheker found records of approximately 250 revolts and conspiracies between 1526 and the end of slavery after the Civil War. Aptheker only counted those whose apparent aim was freedom, involved no less than 10 slaves, and which had been labeled in contemporary references as uprisings, plots, insurrections or any equivalent term. By his own account, the number would be much larger had he used a less strict standard.[2]

The first slave rebellion within the borders of the United States happened in the very first settlement where there were Black slaves. Spanish colonizer Lucas Vásquez de Ayllón founded the settlement in what is now South Carolina in the summer of 1526. Shortly after its establishment, the community of about 500 Spaniards and 100 Black slaves was plagued by death and disease, leading to growing unrest. The neighboring Native Americans grew increasingly suspicious of the settlers.

Several of the slaves finally rebelled around November, joining the Native Americans. When the remnants of the ill-fated Spanish expedition left for Haiti, the former slaves stayed behind as the first permanent, non-indigenous inhabitants of the future United States, together with their newfound Native American friends.[3]

Nat Turner's rebellion in Virginia's Southampton County ranks among the best-known slave uprisings in the United States. When it occurred in 1831, Southampton found itself in economic decline. There was growth of anti-slavery feelings and unrest among the slave population, likely aggravated by precautionary repressive measures devised by the owning class.[4]

Turner, who conducted religious services, had learned how to read and had studied the Bible. His rationale for rebellion featured strong religious language. Turner told other slaves of "visions" and other divine signs signaling them to rise up.

The biblical overtones were only the exterior form of what was essentially a class struggle. Later on, Turner would recount his exchange with a newcomer during a conspiratorial gathering just hours before the revolt. The newcomer declared he had come because

Oppression is coupled with resistance. Nat Turner was a leader in the slave rebellions.

"his life was worth no more than others, and his liberty as dear to him," adding that he would win his freedom or die.

In the evening of Aug. 21, 1831, Turner and another five slaves set out to win their freedom. Turner's master, Joseph Travis, together with his family, were the first to lose their lives to the rebellion. Now with arms and horses, the slaves marched forth, recruiting others along the way. Within the first 24 hours, Turner's group of six slaves swelled to 70.

By the morning of Aug. 23, they had already taken the lives of at least 57 white slave owners and their supporters. On that day, Turner and his followers suffered a severe defeat at the hands of a white militia with superior arms. Three companies of artillery aided by hundreds of other soldiers and militia dealt the final blow the following day, quelling the rebellion through indiscriminate murder.

Although there are indications Turner was a persuasive man, it would be a serious mistake to credit the appeal of the uprising merely to his oratory skills. Aptheker verified the inspirational character of this uprising, writing that it "caused an eruption through the breadth of the slave South—which always rested on a volcano of outraged humanity." The wave of uprisings, inspired by the Nat Turner rebellion, reflected that the oppression of slavery had reached a breaking point—making slave society ripe for rebellion.

FAST FORWARD 260 YEARS: THE L.A. UPRISING

The modern-day United States is in no way an exception to the laws of historical development. Home to the most powerful imperialists in the world, U.S. society is wracked by extreme class contradictions.

Long after the abolition of chattel slavery, racism remains an effective tool of capitalist exploitation. It pits workers against workers on the basis of nationality, allowing the ruling class to "divide and conquer" and super-exploit working people of color.

The racism that pervades U.S. society has more than once triggered massive social convulsions. Hundreds of uprisings took place in African American communities in cities around the country throughout the 1960s.

More recently, the Los Angeles uprising of 1992 illustrates how fundamental contradictions in U.S. society give way to spontaneous uprisings and rebellions.

On March 23, 1991, the Los Angeles Police Department beat Rodney King 56 times with batons, kicked him several times and hogtied him after pursuing him for a traffic violation. King went to the hospital in an ambulance with several cuts and fractures. The beating followed a 15-minute car chase that took place after King failed to pull over, fearful of the police because he was on parole.[5] That might have been the end of it had the whole incident not been caught on video.

King was never charged in connection with the traffic stop. On April 29, 1992, following seven weeks of testimony, a jury of 10 whites, one Latino and one Asian acquitted three of the officers of assault. The racism of the decision could hardly have been more overt.

Within hours, rebellions broke out across Los Angeles. Scores of fires were set and stores were broken into as the community let out its pent-up outrage. The uprising peaked in the next couple of days, lasting about a week. The government responded by declaring martial law and unleashing a wave of repression. No one in the U.S. ruling class had expected such an uprising from the Black community.

RACIST OPPRESSION BREEDS RESISTANCE

People of color experience oppression daily in a multitude of ways: restricted access to education, job discrimination, negative portrayals in the media, hate crimes and the same type of police brutality unleashed upon King—just to name a few. One could easily find a number of overtly racist trials in the U.S. justice system that sparked nothing similar to the reaction to the acquittal of King's attackers. Why, then, did King's case cause such a massive reaction from the oppressed Black community when racism is so pervasive?

The question itself contains the answer.

The L.A. uprising was not simply a reaction to the verdict itself, but rather to the total sum of the racism experienced on a daily basis by the Black community, whose collective consciousness is shaped by their shared experience. The King verdict—itself the result of the oppression of the Black community as a whole—was the spark that set off an explosive situation.

The New York Times reported an exchange that captured the sentiment just outside of the courtroom following the verdict. An African American man shouted, "What race are you?" In response, a white man replied, "I'm an American." "We're not judged as Americans," retorted the Black man.

With these words, he summed up the feeling of the Black community to a verdict that reflected their collective experience as an oppressed nationality.

THE INEVITABILITY OF STRUGGLE

Class society heaps injustice upon injustice, until all of a sudden "one more" such offense turns into chants of "No more!" on the lips of the oppressed. It is the inevitable transformation of quantity into quality.

When these upsurges in the struggle will come, no one knows. What we do know, however, is that they will come. We can say so with the scientific certainty of Marxist analysis backed by countless historical examples.

Rebellion is the natural result of exploitation and oppression. That has been proved over and over again throughout history.

The greatest challenge posed by every instance of rebellion is the need for organization. Nat Turner's conspiracy was too narrow to provide a general framework for rebellion that would go beyond the neighboring plantations. The anti-racist uprising that followed the Rodney King verdicts did not have a leadership that could channel the hatred of the African American community—not just in Los Angeles, but throughout the country—into an effective political force capable of challenging the capitalist state and its racist "justice" system.

The great challenge facing the oppressed and exploited classes in society has never been the willingness to fight back. It has been the ability to organize in a form that can not only fight, but win.

That task—turning rebellion into revolution—has been one of the main contributions of revolutionary communism and underlines the need for a communist party. □

Endnotes

1. Herbert Aptheker, American Negro Slave Revolts. 5th Edition. International Publishers, New York, 1983 (1943). pp. 143-145.
2. Ibid. p. 162
3. Ibid. p 163
4. Ibid. pp. 294-295
5. New York Times, April 30, 1992.

Workers and oppressed take center stage

What difference can a socialist revolution make?

B ETWEEN 5,000 and 10,000 years ago, human societies in different parts of the world split into classes. Social classes are defined by social and economic positions in society relative to the creation of wealth in society, as well as the interrelations among these groupings.

The emergence of classes corresponded roughly to the development of agricultural and herding societies, where for the first time surplus goods were created. Prior to that, humans lived in hunter-gatherer arrangements characterized by extreme scarcity. The appropriation of the surplus by one part of the population at the expense of others laid the basis for the division of society into classes.

Karl Marx and Frederick Engels were among the first to see the struggle between these classes as the driving force of history. One class organizes society to subjugate the others—Marx and Engels pointed to this as the emergence of the state as an organ of repression. On the other hand, the exploited classes struggle against the ruling class, often ending up in an eruption of open violence.

For that reason, every society's history is punctuated by revolutions—an eruption of violent class struggle that results in the overturning of the power of one class in favor of another.

Class struggle is like a tug-of-war between the corresponding forces. Either the old social, economic and political order is preserved, or the old order is eradicated and fundamental change occurs as a new society takes its place.

Slaves of antiquity, serfs under feudal rule, capitalism's wage workers—indeed, every known oppressed class in history—instinctively rebels against its oppression. By the same token, the oppressors that hold their victims in bondage do everything possible to maintain their privileged social position and retain political power. This is so part of day-to-day life that often the participants—especially the oppressed—are not even conscious of this struggle.

Revolutionary Marxists aim to study the objective laws of class struggle throughout history in order to prepare for socialist revolution in the modern era. That involves a comprehensive understanding of the class character of revolutions in past historical periods that brought to power new forms of class domination.

REVOLUTIONS—FOR A FEW

Capitalist rule was solidified by a series of revolutions in Europe between the 16th and the 19th centuries. The merchant and property-owning classes began accumulating wealth under the political rule of the feudal lords. The bourgeoisie developed ideologically and culturally long before seizing absolute control of the state. They gained expertise in various fields like the arts and military science, ultimately indispensable for spreading influence and retaining power once in charge.

While today's capitalist ruling class grew in wealth and social power in the cracks of feudal society, the oppressed masses did not have that advantage. In fact, under capitalism, they have grown less and less powerful.

Yet it was this class, always constituting the majority of society, which was the decisive factor in the success of the bourgeois revolutions. During the 1789 French Revolution or during Latin America's 19th-century wars for independence, slaves, indentured servants, peasants and workers were the combatants in the battles that allowed a privileged class to obtain political power.

The bourgeois revolutions were authentically revolutionary because they elevated society to a higher level of humanity, developing society's productive forces and tearing away the backward prejudices of feudal lords and priests. But these revolutions did not aim to eradicate exploitation and privilege. On the contrary, the bourgeois-democratic revolutions' central objective was to expand "bourgeois right": the freedom of the owning class to exploit and trade without restriction.

Up until the modern era, revolutions were led by representatives of property-owning classes, whose political skills are the product of social privilege. The oppressed masses did not possess the skills that come with knowledge of politics—simply because their oppression included being denied any political involvement.

In general, the oppressed masses were not aware of the ultimate aims of the bourgeois-democratic revolutions. They were drawn in by the hope of freedom, however loosely defined that was. The rising capitalist class used demagoguery from the start, using slogans of "freedom" and "equality" to appeal to the non-privileged sectors of society.

Despite the fact that the oppressed classes were not the main beneficiaries of past revolutions, they were usually the ones willing to make harsh sacrifices by taking on the burden of fighting revolutions. The soon-to-be ruling classes benefited from the instinctive rebelliousness of oppressed and exploited people.

> *The socialist revolution is the first example where the most exploited class consciously fights for its own interests.*

It was poor farmers who served under George Washington in the American Revolutionary War for Independence. Many of these same forces took up arms against the newly formed U.S. government during Shay's Rebellion of 1786-87.

African Americans fought valiantly during the Civil War. Yet after the war and despite the promise of Reconstruction, they continued to suffer from racist discrimination and terror.

The bourgeois-democratic revolution in Europe was the rising capitalist class' response to economic developments that awakened mass resentment towards feudalism. But lacking class consciousness, an essential component for addressing their class interest, the exploited masses of peasants and small craftspeople were consumed by the events of that period and followed the lead of alien class forces.

THE WORKERS' REVOLUTION

Unlike revolutions of past epochs, the socialist revolution aims to place the working class—a propertyless, oppressed class—in the position of ruling class. This class has not been accumulating wealth as it builds its bid for power. On the contrary, the working class as a class owns less wealth every year. Its members every day lose more benefits and access to education.

Socialist revolution presumes the consciousness and self-awareness of the oppressed masses. The socialist revolution is the first example where the most exploited class consciously fights for its own interests. The socialist revolution ultimately aims not to enhance the traditions of privilege or uphold the system of profits, but to abolish "bourgeois right" by revolutionary measures.

For this reason, revolutionaries in the United States and around the world have great confidence that the working and oppressed masses will rally to take up the cause for the socialist revolution as their own.

The oppressors would no longer be the beneficiaries of the vast wealth created by the labor of working people. Nor would they enjoy the many freedoms to exploit and oppress the majority to which they were accustomed. They would be stripped of every means to safeguard their domination over the social and economic life of society.

The accumulated wealth stored in the capitalists' banks will be seized and converted to public ownership in the custody of the socialist state. Private ownership of the means of production, transportation, commerce, land, water and everything that under capitalism exists for the private benefit of wealthy families, would be outlawed. The hundreds of billions of dollars spent on corporate subsidies, one of the most blatant forms of thievery the rulers exercise, would also be banned and added to the resources freed for the benefit of the whole.

Cuban doctors' acts of international solidarity are examples of what is possible.

PHOTO: BILL HACKWELL

WHAT CAN BE GAINED?

It is this socialist revolution, carried out with the conscious participation of the working class and guided by the interests of the vast majority, that opens the door to a society without exploitation.

Based on the socialist revolution's bold measures, oppressed and working people for the first time stand to be the main beneficiaries of a fundamental reorganization of society. Especially in a rich and highly developed capitalist country like the United States, where technology has developed the means of production to the highest level ever known in history, once-hoarded resources will no longer sit idle in warehouses waiting to rot. These resources will be able to be utilized in unimaginable ways to benefit society.

Every socialist revolution from 1917 began with two priorities. One was defending the revolution from imperialist-backed armed counterrevolution. The other priority was to urgently begin addressing the human needs of the working classes and of all society.

The construction of hospitals and other types of healthcare facilities; grade schools and universities for the education of the young and for the elevation of workers' technical levels in every field; homes and apartment complexes in order for working-class families to have decent housing; improving and expanding the infrastructure to enable rapid industrial development; improving transportation to further secure the food supply of society—all these became the priority.

By removing profit considerations as the motive for decisions, public works can be improved. Unemployment, homelessness, hunger and poverty can be systematically eliminated.

The funds and resources that under capitalism are wasted on private profits for the super-rich would then become available for training vast numbers of medical doctors, scientists, engineers, craftspeople and experts. Because all areas of social and economic life are free to develop, the role of education becomes primary—along with a new respect for learning.

All of the socialist governments were required to take emergency measures due to civil wars and problems caused by foreign threats, economic blockades and sanctions. These emergency measures, some of which included restoring elements of capitalism, were motivated by the need to survive in a hostile world. Each retreat away from socialism led to defects and deformations. Moreover, as is the case with China, the reintroduction of capitalist market mechanisms was not always a temporary and imposed retreat but a policy decision by the ruling communist party.

Although it would be foolhardy to hold up any socialist government as "the model" for the future, it would be an act of deceit and treachery to fail to understand the achievements of the socialist revolutions where they occurred. Were it not for the experiences of socialist construction in the Soviet Union, China, Korea, Cuba and many others, discussing this could be considered wild speculation. Instead, it is the record of socialist revolution.

What is more, that record has taken place in societies plagued by scarcity and underdevelopment. Imagine the possibilities with a revolution in a developed country like the United States! The scarcity of basic necessities could be replaced by abundance. No longer will people have to fight for what they need, because accessibility to needed resources becomes one of the norms of a society founded on cooperation and solidarity.

Under conditions of abundance and social equality, competition among workers—under capitalism the cause of so many crimes— could be addressed. The new material conditions of economic abundance along with a new mass education campaign rooted in class solidarity will permit a revolutionary transformation of the general culture and human relations. It would open the door to eradicating the poisons of racism, sexism and anti-LGBT hatred.

For all these reasons, the socialist revolution is like none other in history.

But none of this can happen without revolution. Making that revolution a reality requires the creation of an organization that is committed to leading the charge in uprooting capitalist exploitation and raising the level of class consciousness to meet the challenges ahead. ☐

Don't stop with reforms!

'Reaching beyond the existing social order' to revolution

MILLIONS of people in the United States understand the problems of capitalist society: poverty, unemployment, racism, war or any other of the many other social ills that working-class people face.

Hundreds of thousands of those, if asked, would sincerely like to see social change to address those problems.

Yet communist ideas are still a small factor in U.S. working-class consciousness.

Talking about how to make a revolution in the United States does not always generate the kind of fear and anti-communist hatred that has been the case during periods of witch hunts and red-baiting—at least among most social justice activists. Rather, the biggest criticism of communist politics among activists is that it is unrealistic, hopeless or not practical.

"When the revolution happens, I'll be with you," communist organizers have heard countless times. "But for now, I'm going to focus on helping my community."

The speaker could be a union organizer, a volunteer at a women's shelter, an anti-war activist or any other of the thousands of people who selflessly sacrifice countless hours trying to improve the lives of poor and working people. With these dedicated activists, communists do not try to engage in long-winded arguments about the need for revolution. Instead, they show themselves to be the most dedicated fighters in the many struggles for workers' rights, for women's rights, and against war and racism.

Sometimes, however, the pragmatic argument against revolution takes a political form. A politician or political party holds out the possibility of reforming capitalism to the point where people's needs can be addressed without revolution and without infringing on the ruling class' right to exploit and rule. This is known as reformism, and it is one of the main poisons in the working-class movement.

Reformists do not always come across as misleaders. They often present themselves as advancing a "progressive" agenda. Sometimes they might even pose as contributing to breaking the two-party hold on political power in the United States.

Despite all this, revolutionary Marxism has considered these forces a danger that inhibits working-class consciousness. Lenin wrote in 1913, "Unlike the anarchists, the Marxists recognize struggle for reforms, i.e., for measures that improve the conditions [of] the working people without destroying the power of the ruling class. At the same time, however, the Marxists wage a most resolute struggle against the reformists, who, directly or indirectly, restrict the aims and activities of the working class to the winning of reforms. Reformism is bourgeois deception of the workers, who, despite individual improvements, will always remain wage-slaves, as long as there is the domination of capital."

U.S. REFORMISM: 'LESSER OF TWO EVILS'

Reformism in the United States comes in many varieties. By far the most common version is the line that the only way poor and working people—especially African Americans—can get a political voice is through the Democratic Party. The misnamed and reformist Communist Party USA consistently argues for supporting Democratic candidates as a way to "defeat the right" and build a "labor-led people's movement."

The Democratic Party, "a class-based party," is "the only election instrument that is capable of defeating the extreme right at this moment in the electoral arena," the CPUSA argues.[1] It refers to the 2008 elections, but it could have been written during any election year over the past 70 years. CPUSA lists "a decisive Democratic Party landslide at the Presidential and Congressional levels" as the first condition for a "decisive victory" over the "extreme right," by which it means the Republican Party.

This line, designed to give a left veneer to a fundamentally reformist line, is repeated in certain sectors of the liberal political movement and national union leadership. This line has become more and more untenable as the Democrats support funding Bush's war in Iraq, while joining the chorus of threats against Iran. In spite of receiving tens of millions of dollars in union funds, it was the Democrats under Clinton who passed NAFTA and kicked 7 million children off welfare.

More and more people are looking for a way out of supporting pro-war, anti-working-class and pro-corporate Democratic politicians as a "lesser of two evils."

U.S. REFORMISM: THE GREEN PARTY

Another form of reformism in the U.S. political arena is the Green Party of the United States, which presents itself as a federation of state parties "committed to environmentalism, non-violence, social justice and grassroots organizing."[2] Many hard-working and committed progressive activists have affiliated with the Green Party. It presents itself as an alternative to the two parties of the ruling class. While the Green Party presents itself as a party of activists, it sees this activism as "building the support networks needed to run candidates for local office first, followed by higher offices later."[3]

The Green Party achieved national attention during the 2000 elections when their candidate, consumer advocate Ralph Nader, won 2.9 million votes. Nader's votes exceeded George Bush's margin of victory over Al Gore in several states including Florida. This provoked hysteria among "lesser of two evils" advocates, blaming the Greens for Bush's victory and conveniently ignoring Gore's right-wing electoral campaign and the Democrat's loss of credibility among millions.

Although many of its members are anti-capitalist, the Green Party is not an anti-capitalist party. Their "Ten Key Values," which are "guiding principles" and not a binding program, promote restructuring society "away from a system which is controlled by and mostly benefits the powerful few." But nowhere does it challenge the right of those powerful few to own or rule.

During the 2008 elections, the Greens are positioning themselves as an anti-war party, taking advantage of the fact that Democratic and Republican candidates alike solidly oppose an immediate end to the war in Iraq. In a Jan. 24, 2008, press release, they criticize pro-Democratic "anti-war" organizations like MoveOn.org for "setting back the peace movement" by backing Democratic candidates. "Groups like MoveOn that divert the energies of peace activists towards Democrat candidates who fail to push for a prompt and total withdrawal only undermine the peace movement and advance the war agenda," one of their candidates stated in the release. "Voters need genuine peace candidates like those from the Green Party."

SETTING THE RECORD STRAIGHT

Neither the social-democratic "lesser of two evils" reformism nor the newer Green Party version of selling reform while rejecting the need for revolution are unique to the United States. Social-democratic parties have been ruling parties across Europe and even at times in the United States. Capitalist exploitation is still rampant on either side of the Atlantic. The need for reform is still as burning as before the reformists took power.

Since the overthrow of the Soviet Union, the Greens have become more of a factor on the European scene. In 1998, the German Green Party joined the Social Democrats in a ruling coalition government. The German Greens, currently known as the Alliance 90/Greens, are affiliated with the same "Global Green Network" as the Green Party of the United States.

The Green parties emerged in Europe in the 1970s. They stood to the right of the overall social movements that were developing at that time. Just a few years before, socialists and workers had been on the verge of revolution in France in 1968. The Greens emphasized a non-class-struggle approach to environmentalism, focusing on getting capitalism to adjust its destructive "policies" that harmed the environment. This had a particular appeal to the middle classes and the more liberal bourgeoisie who were rightfully alarmed about pending ecological catastrophe.

The German Greens were the first Green Party to elect a representative to office. They had been founded in 1979 in what was then West Germany. At that time, the German Democratic Republic in eastern Germany was part of the socialist camp.

In 1983 the Greens won their first major governmental posts in the German parliament. They had greater electoral successes through the 1980s, fueled by ecological concerns and nuclear disarmament. The Pentagon and NATO stored nuclear missiles at West German bases.

It was in this setting that Joschka Fischer, who would later become prime minister, became the leading figure in the German Green Party.

In the 1990s, the Greens maintained their presence in the German legislature thanks to their merger with Alliance 90, an East German anti-communist formation. Alliance 90 was a coalition of so-called human rights organizations including New Forum, Democracy Now, and Initiative for Peace and Human Rights. Alliance 90 was part of the movement that fomented the overthrow of socialism in East Germany.

'Reformism is bourgeois deception of the workers, who, despite individual improvements, will always remain wage-slaves, as long as there is the domination of capital.' —V.I. Lenin

During this period, Green politics moved more quickly to the right. Leftist party members quit in 1990 and 1991, unable to halt the right-wing direction of the party's reformist orientation.

As early as 1994, prominent Green Party leaders like Joshcka Fischer and Jens Reich called for the privatization of state-owned utilities, social services and the cutting of social programs. These leaders are part of the same current whose "Key Values" in the United States supposedly include restructuring society "away from" the interests of a "powerful few."

As if that was not enough, in 1993 the leadership of the party endorsed the idea of "humanitarian intervention in foreign lands." This broke with the anti-military sentiment that had dominated German mass consciousness after the crimes of Hitler's Nazis in World War II. The Greens managed to reverse a taboo that the right in Germany could not.

GREENS IN POWER: PRO-WAR, ANTI-WORKER

In 1998, the Green Party joined the Social Democrats in forming the federal government. Joschka Fischer, the leader of the Greens, became the vice chancellor and foreign minister.

Spurred on by Fischer's pro-war policies, the Green Party supported German imperialism and NATO's military campaign against

Yugoslavia in their Second Extraordinary Assembly of Federal Delegates of May 1999. In a resolution reeking of imperial arrogance and filled with blame-the-victim hypocrisy, the Greens wrote, "The decision whether to support or reject intervention in Yugoslavia against the degrading policies of the Yugoslav government must for most of us have been the most difficult political decision ever. Many have come to realize that the point cannot be to decide which principle of Green policy has a higher priority: safeguarding and protecting human rights or declaring one's adherence to pacifism and anti-militarism."

It was the worst form of demagoguery, hiding the fact that it was German imperialism that was largely to blame for Yugoslavia's civil war by financing and arming the anti-communist secessionist movements in Slovenia and Croatia. "Human rights" became the false slogan for a vicious NATO air campaign that included dropping 23,000 bombs and missiles on a defenseless country.

The Green Party, while it shared political power, gave the green light to sending German troops to Afghanistan, Congo, Kuwait, East Timor, Macedonia, Sudan and Mozambique. German imperialism is now one of the largest suppliers of "peacekeeping" troops worldwide.

PHOTO: BILL HACKWELL

Every year, anti-war activists hold demonstrations in Germany, a tradition that dates back to the 1960s. In 2007, the Green Party for the first time withheld their support. Green Party leader Claudia Roth railed against the demonstrations, accusing them of having "a black and white view" and a "blanket rejection of the military."

Needless to say, the party is now far more popular among the wealthy than the working class. According to a Jan. 25, 2008, Infratest Dimap research report, higher-income voters (earning more than $4,500 per month) vote Green more than lower-income voters. Greens get 10 percent of the vote among managers and the self-employed, but only 5 percent among workers and the unemployed.

In the end, it was the Green Party as a junior partner with their Social Democratic allies that was able to preside over privatizations, cuts in social programs and workers' rights and the once-taboo military reactivation of German troops on foreign soil. The right wing would have endured mass protests and political opposition in many corners, including the massive German labor movement, had they tried to do this. But the German ruling class found better marketers. This is where the road of reformism leads.

REFORM OR REVOLUTION?

The relation between the struggles for reform and for revolution has been the source of major differences within the Marxist movement since the 19th century. Writing in "Social Reform or Revolution" in 1900, Rosa Luxemburg stated, "It is not true that socialism will arise automatically from the daily struggle of the working class. Socialism will be the consequence of (1), the growing contradictions of capitalist economy and (2), of the comprehension by the working class of the unavailability of the suppression of these contradictions through a social transformation.

"When, in the manner of revisionism, the first condition is denied and the second rejected, the labor movement finds itself reduced to a simple co-operative and reformist movement. We move here in a straight line toward the total abandonment of the class viewpoint."

Luxemburg was responding to German socialist-reformist Eduard Bernstein, who argued that capitalism could be peacefully transformed to socialism—as long as people were active. He theorized that by means such as the creation of a credit system, the expansion of modern communications, the further stratification of production and the growth of the middle class, capitalist crises could be eliminated. Eventually, Bernstein thought, the practical goals of the workers for better conditions and a better life would be met. "The final goal, no matter what it is, is nothing," he argued. "The movement is everything."

Luxemburg explained how what may be a powerful mass movement can end with nothing without the tools of Marxism and the struggle for power by the working class. She explained, "The union of the broad popular masses with an aim reaching beyond the existing social order, the union of the daily struggle with the great world transformation, that is the task of the Social-Democratic movement, which must logically grope on its road of development between the following two rocks: abandoning the mass character of the party or abandoning its final aim, falling into bourgeois reformism or into sectarianism, anarchism or opportunism."

It is the combining of these two elements—being with the masses of working people in the struggles for jobs and housing, against war and racism, for health care and all the other reforms that are so badly needed on the one hand, and constantly aiming for destroying the capitalist class and its system of exploitation on the other—that is the greatest test for those who hope to achieve social justice.

It is the historic task of communism and the historic goal of the working class. □

Endnotes

1. Sam Webb, "On the road again: Challenges and opportunities in the 2008 elections," www.cpusa.org/filemanager/download/83/new.pdf.
2. Green Party USA, "About Us," www.gp.org/about.shtml.
3. "A Brief History of the Green Party," www.gp.org.history.shtml.

Anarchism's track record

What is militancy without a winning program?

I N the struggle for a better world, the working-class movement often faces the question: Which way forward?

It may be in a strike, where the bosses are threatening to bring in scabs. It may be in a demonstration, when the cops are preparing to disperse the crowd. Or it may be in the heat of street battles, with the government on the verge of collapse.

Workers organize to have a way of making those decisions in the heat of battle. In the class struggle, a moment's vacillation can make the difference between success and failure.

It is also the basis for political theory. Revolutionary theory or ideology in particular is the distilled lessons of the struggles of oppressed people throughout history, especially the lessons of the working class and oppressed people against capitalism and imperialism.

Marxism, or revolutionary socialism, emerged soon after the birth of the modern working class itself. But it was not the only revolutionary ideology to emerge in the course of the class struggle.

Anarchism grew up alongside socialism in the working-class movement in Europe in the 19th century. Almost unrecognizable from its proponents today, most of whom have only been attracted to cultural or lifestyle trends attributed to the movement, anarchism at one time had deep roots in the revolutionary working-class movement.

From the outset, anarchism was a revolutionary ideology. It stood for the end of the capitalist system and for a new society free from exploitation.

Like communists, anarchists recognize that the capitalist system, founded on brutal exploitation, must be overthrown. Like revolutionary Marxists, they oppose reformist and pacifist illusions that the capitalist state can be gradually or peacefully transformed into something that can benefit the working class.

Yet on a few fundamental questions—questions related to the way forward—anarchism and communism part ways.

Anarchism is not a homogeneous theory or practice. Different movements in different parts of the world have called themselves or have been called anarchist despite divergent perspectives. However, most currents of anarchism share some basic similarities. Anarchism advocates the destruction of the capitalist system in order to realize a classless society. Anarchism wholly rejects the role of the state as an institution of force and violence against the majority of society. It rejects political action—voting, lobbying, or appealing to politicians—as a means of achieving revolution.

ORIGINS OF ANARCHISM

Among the first to describe anarchism as a political philosophy was Pierre-Joseph Proudhon. In his 1840 pamphlet "What is Property?"—he answered, "Property is theft." This had a significant impact on the growing radical movement. When Karl Marx met Proudhon in Paris, he challenged him on several key points, especially his belief in "mutualism," that the primary role of the worker is as an individual producer with property rights to what was produced.

Despite Proudhon's clearly petty-bourgeois schemes, his critique of capitalist society won many supporters in France. During the 1871 Paris Commune, the first seizure of power by the working class, his supporters played key roles in both the successes and the defeats.

In 1864, a number of socialist and working-class organizations united to form the International Workers' Association—the First International. The IWA held its first congress in 1866 in Geneva, Switzerland. It was a coalition among working-class forces representing a variety of political and philosophical viewpoints. Marx was among the founding and leading members.

The members of the IWA were not merely political theorists. They were engaged in the revolutions of the mid-1800s. Proudhon's Mutualists were represented. So were representatives of the militant Chartist trade-union movement from England.

In 1868, Russian revolutionist Mikhail Bakunin joined the IWA. Bakunin was a veteran of countless revolutionary struggles and had served time in the Czarist prisons. He had been the first to translate Marx's "Capital" into Russian. But his views on political action were more in keeping with Proudhon than Marx.

Bakunin and his supporters in the First International argued against socialists taking part in elections. Marx and his supporters advocated participation in bourgeois elections as an opportunity to unite the working class politically and on a class basis. In 1872, after fierce debates on the subject, the majority in the IWA expelled Bakunin and his supporters.

Bakunin opened a wider criticism of Marxism, arguing in particular against the dictatorship of the proletariat and counterposing the "spontaneous federation of communes," local collectives of workers and peasants who would govern themselves and coordinate on a federation level.

"A fundamental division arises between the socialists and revolutionary collectivists [anarchists] on the one hand and the authoritarian communists [Marxists] on the other," Bakunin wrote in the 1871 pamphlet, "The Paris Commune and the Idea of the State." "The difference is only that the communists imagine they can attain their goal by the development and organization of political power of the working classes. ... The revolutionary socialists [anarchists], on the other hand, believe they can succeed only through the development of the non-political and anti-political social power of the working classes in the city and country."

In summary, Bakunin and other anarchists counterposed "direct action"—in some cases strikes, in other cases individual attacks against bosses and politicians—to the "political" work of organizing legally into political parties. They rejected outright the possibility of workers creating their own state to defend their gains in the course of revolution, arguing that it would inevitably become a tool of repression against the workers themselves.

U.S. ANARCHISM: SOCIALISTS AND WOBBLIES

The split in the First International was reflected within the working-class movements around the world. In most countries, one or another wing dominated: Socialism in Germany, anarchism in Spain and Italy. One place where both wings organized side-by-side, if in competition, was the United States.

On the one hand, the Socialists spread radical anti-capitalist consciousness far and wide across the country. They played a leading role in the 1877 railway strikes and dozens of other smaller strikes. By 1912, they had over 1,000 elected Socialist officeholders in 337 towns and cities.[1] In 1917, they had some 80,000 members.[2] Its most prominent leader, Eugene Debs, received nearly 1 million votes when he ran for president in 1920 while he was in prison for opposing World War I.

On the other hand, the Industrial Workers of the World held its founding convention in June 1905 in Chicago. Bill Haywood, the general secretary of the Western Federation of Miners, opened the founding convention of "Wobblies," as IWW members were known, saying, "This is the Continental Congress of the working class. We are here to confederate the workers of this country into a working-class movement that shall have for its purpose the emancipation of the working class from the slave bondage of capitalism." The IWW was a revolutionary labor movement that viewed the organization of industrial unions as a means to reach a goal—that of working-class revolution.

The IWW came from the anarchist tradition of the Haymarket struggle for the eight-hour day in Chicago in 1886. They led the famous 1912 "Bread and Roses" strike in Lawrence, Mass., as well as major strikes of silk workers in Patterson, N.J., in 1913 and iron miners in Minnesota in 1916. Some of the most outspoken workers' leaders in the turn-of-the-century United States were Wobblies: Bill Haywood, Elizabeth Gurley Flynn, Joe Hill, Mother Jones, Emma Goldman and many others.

Both the Socialists and the IWW were part of a general radicalization of the U.S. working class. Both had failures as well as successes, even on their own terms. The Socialist Party's emphasis on electoral politics gave rise to a right-wing opportunist wing, epitomized by New York City's Morris Hillquit, a racist and pro-war "socialist." The IWW's rejection of what they called class-collaborationist union contracts led to short-lived gains, like the fact that most of the gains from their most successful strike in Lawrence were lost within the next two years.

THE RUSSIAN REVOLUTION

For as long as no decisive event impacted the working-class movement, the struggle between anarchists and socialists was largely in the realm of theory. On a world scale, both movements registered successes and failures as in the United States.

The decisive event that tipped the balance forever in favor of the Marxists was the 1917 Russian Revolution led by V.I. Lenin and the Bolshevik Party. Lenin's Bolsheviks had practiced a form of revolutionary Marxism that was unlike the experience of the mass socialist parties of Western Europe. It blended the militant class warfare of the anarchists with the political action that characterized the Marxists.

The victory of the Russian Bolsheviks electrified workers and oppressed people across the world. It served as a pole of attraction for revolutionaries of many different political backgrounds. For example, in the United States, James Cannon, who had been an IWW organizer, was an original member at the 1921 founding convention of the Workers Party—the predecessor of the Communist Party. Also in attendance at the convention were Charles Ruthenberg, a Socialist, and William Foster, a former IWW organizer who had joined the more

The 1917 victory of Lenin and the Bolshevik Party in
Russia tilted the balance against anarchism.

PHOTO: ZUMA PRESS

reformist American Federation of Labor unions. These were the first leaders of the Communist movement in the United States.

The gain for communism was a loss for anarchism and reformist socialism. Historian Theodore Draper notes that by 1925, "The Socialist Labor Party vegetated hopelessly. The IWW was no more than a shell of its old self and only 11 delegates attended its 1925 convention. The Socialist Party, its historian says ... 'did very little to attract the attention of the general public.' The AFL had sunk into a decade-long torpor, its leaders blissfully oblivious to a dwindling membership and far more interested in imitating capitalism than organizing against it."[3]

A similar realignment of forces took place around the world.

In Russia itself, anarchists had very little political space, since the Bolsheviks were implementing a policy of empowering the workers and building a state in their interests. The few scattered attempts by anarchists or anarchist-influenced movements to oppose the new Soviet government "from the left"—the Makhno movement after 1920 and the Kronstadt mutiny in 1921—won virtually no support from the broader working class.

THE SPANISH CIVIL WAR

The Spanish revolution and civil war of the 1930s was the last test of anarchism in practice.

Throughout the late 1800s and early 1900s, Spanish peasants and workers were engaged in almost constant struggle. Felix Morrow describes the beginning of this period well: "Four major revolutions before 1875, followed by four white terrors, were merely crescendos in an almost continuous tune of peasant revolts and army mutinies."

Spain entered the world capitalist depression of the 1930s with a somewhat industrialized, somewhat feudal economy. Spain was far less developed than its counterparts in Europe. The capitalist class was allied with the monarchy, tied to feudal landholding roots and the reactionary Catholic Church hierarchy. The great majority of the population was tied to the land.

The anarcho-syndicalist National Labor Confederation (CNT) was the largest trade-union federation with 1.5 million members in 1931. It was also the most militant. The socialist General Workers Union (UGT) had several hundred thousand members. The

Communist Party was relatively small, largely because it had formed after the CNT and the Socialists, both of which had respected and revolutionary traditions in the Spanish working class.

Mass protests, after the depression broke out, toppled dictator Gen. Miguel Primo de Rivera in 1930. Right-wing monarchist parties were soundly defeated in elections in 1931. The hopes of the masses were high.

When the republican government began to put down strikes and demonstrations, working-class mobilizations increased. General strikes took place in 1931 and 1934. Workers were seizing factories throughout the country.

In July 1936, Gen. Francisco Franco staged a coup with the support of the entire military and the Spanish ruling class. The workers' organizations—anarchists, socialists and communists—distributed arms to defend themselves. For the next three years, the class struggle would take place in the streets and fields.

The anarchists had the strongest base in the working class. They had more workers under arms. Their program of direct action and putting power in the hands of the working class directly now had a chance of being realized. In some places, it was—at least initially.

In Catalonia, and especially in its capital city of Barcelona, workers took key government buildings and expropriated factories. The power really was in the hands of the workers.

But in September 1936, the anarchists joined the "democratic" capitalists in the republican government. They did so in the name of unity against Franco's fascism—but it was unity behind a bourgeois program at the expense of their own program of workers' power.

The results were catastrophic. The anarchist-led militias were disbanded. Despite more than two years of heroic fighting on the part of tens of thousands of workers from Spain and around the world, the bourgeois republican government surrendered to Franco in March 1939.

It would be unfair to put the loss of the Spanish Civil War at the feet of the anarchists. By that time, the Third Communist International had adopted the non-revolutionary "popular front" program of the Stalin leadership in the Soviet Union that pursued accommodation with the "democratic" capitalists out of lack of faith in the working class. This orientation crippled the Communist leadership in Spain.

The fact remains: The leadership of the largest anarchist movement since the Russian Revolution proved itself unable to guide the Spanish workers to victory at the moment when their power was greatest. At the decisive moment, the worshipping of trade unionism, even of the most militant form, bowed its head to political leadership, even of the most opportunistic form.

The price of defeat was heavy. Spain suffered under the fascist dictatorship of Francisco Franco until 1975.

ANARCHISM TODAY

Today, the anarchist movement is a mere shadow of its historical self. Contemporary anarchism is primarily a cultural practice that glorifies individualism and is entirely divorced from the working-class movement.

Cultural anarchism intersects and diverges with a more militant contemporary strain of anarchism—itself also divorced from the working-class movement—that engages in isolated direct action against the manifestations of capitalism. It is loosely organized in affiliated groups that operate on the consensus of all present—with no consideration for experience, affirmative action, or class consciousness—that lends itself extremely well to police infiltration. Contemporary anarchism claims to reject any form of leadership as authoritarian—but its organizational form lends itself to the institutionalization of leadership by those who appoint themselves as such.

This form of anarchism, with no roots whatsoever in the working class, thrived for a short time after the destruction of the Soviet Union in the anti-globalization movement. The anti-globalization movement centered around high-profile, somewhat large-scale and loosely organized actions against the meetings of global capital, represented by the World Trade Organization, the World Bank, the International Monetary Fund and the G8.

The anti-globalization movement engaged in street tactics that appealed to many as an answer to the destructive march of capital, unfettered by the obstacle of the socialist camp. It drew militant workers and young people into a series of battles against the cops who protected the capitalists.

Many organizations and individuals participated in that movement over two years, although the anarchists were the dominant force. Yet within days of the Sept. 11, 2001 attacks, the anti-globalization movement in the United States dissipated. The movement lacked the organization and leadership with a long-term perspective towards struggle against the capitalist class using all available means. Because of this, the intense pressure of the ruling-class reaction to the Sept.11, 2001 attacks overcame the anti-globalization movement. Its leaders did nothing in reaction to the racist attacks at home and drive toward war abroad. An explicitly anti-imperialist wing of the U.S. anti-globalization movement that included Marxists in the leadership quickly adjusted its tactics and slogans to launch the ANSWER Coalition–Act Now to Stop War and End Racism. That movement quickly forged alliances with the Arab-American and Muslim communities and revived a street-based mass movement that pushed back against the dominant pro-war hysteria that had swept the United States. Within a few months the anarchist leadership quickly withered and virtually vanished inside the U.S.

The same militancy that once won anarchism the respect of millions of workers still has an attraction for many youth who want to fight the system. It has been the responsibility of revolutionary communists since Lenin to match that militancy and at the same time to provide a program for victory. □

Endnotes

1. Cannon, James, "The First 10 Years of American Communism," Pathfinder, 1962, p. 260.
2. Draper, Theodor, "American Communism and Soviet Russia," Vintage, 1986, p. 18.
3. Ibid, p. 150.

Socialism and the legacy of the Soviet Union

THE single biggest event that shaped global politics in the 20th century was the Russian Revolution of 1917, which gave birth to the Soviet Union. The first socialist government's existence was the pivot for world events in history's most turbulent and dynamic century. The destruction of the Soviet Union 74 years later in 1991 has been the dominant factor shaping global politics in the nearly 17 years since.

Karl Marx and Frederick Engels wrote in 1848, "A specter is haunting Europe—the specter of communism." However haunting the specter of communism may have appeared to the European bourgeoisie in the mid-1800s, it would seem mild compared to the undiluted hysteria directed by all the imperialist powers and old ruling classes against the actually-existing Soviet Union throughout the 20th century.

The victory of the Russian Revolution transformed the presentation of communism from an idea or an ideology into a living, breathing social and political experience. It was an attempt to consciously build a society based on the interests and needs of the working classes.

Communism's new identification with a state power was extremely positive for the world communist movement. The domestic programs, the radical reorganization of constitutional law and the revolutionary foreign policy of the new Soviet state spread the appeal of communism to nearly every corner of the globe. Millions of people were drawn into political life and the communist movement as the idea of workers' power took on flesh and bones.

In the colonized world, the Soviet message of self-determination and freedom drew the most advanced youth directly into newly founded communist parties. From China to Vietnam to South Africa, the banner of Soviet communism became synonymous not just with socialism but with the aspirations for national independence.

As the influence of communism spread throughout the 20th century to all corners of the world, every capitalist power brought to bear the weight of its media, politicians, universities and especially armies in a global struggle to counter Soviet influence.

The identification of communism with a state power expanded later to its political association with the governments in Eastern Europe, China, North Korea, Vietnam and Cuba, along with newly founded revolutionary governments in Africa that were also trying to take a socialist road. Communism became inseparably connected to what was known as the "socialist bloc" governments. As the first, largest and most powerful socialist power, the Soviet Union was identified as the anchor of this global camp.

POLITICS, IDEOLOGY AND STATE POWER

Conflating the historical ideology and perspective of communism with a government or a bloc of governments also created a tremendous disadvantage, in spite of the material advantages that came from possessing state power. Every setback, weakness, retreat, defect and deformation suffered by the Soviet Union was also identified as an inherent negative feature of communism.

That the socialist revolutions took place in poor countries instead of the rich imperialist countries gave the capitalist propaganda machine ready-made ammunition to argue against socialism. Anti-communist literature could point to the relative affluence of the imperialist countries and assert, "Socialism or communism is nothing but the equality of poverty for the people while 'officials' and 'bureaucrats' enjoy privileges based on their association with the ruling communist party."

This same anti-communist propaganda, spoon-fed to the people of the United States, obscured and falsified every real social and economic achievement made by the Soviet Union, China or Cuba. Nowhere was it mentioned that every Soviet worker had a legal right to a job, free health care and free child care. Rent was a small fraction of income. Every worker was guaranteed one month of paid vacation.

These social rights were maligned or hidden in the West. In every instance, the propaganda emphasized that the capitalist United States was rich and affluent, with ordinary workers having access to all sorts of goods and services that were not accessible in the Soviet Union.

When the Soviet Union was overthrown in 1991, capitalist propaganda highlighted one theme: The collapse of the Soviet Union meant that communism itself was now dead. The dream of poor and working people was vanquished forever. "The end of history," was the theme of a best seller in 1992 written by academic Francis Fukuyama. The essence of this argument was that capitalism and the rule by a class of billionaires of and over society was the natural order of things.

NO ANTI-COMMUNIST UPRISING

The Soviet Union was not overthrown by foreign military intervention. Nor was it brought down by an uprising of discontented workers as happened with the October 1917 revolution. In fact, nine months before its dissolution, 77 percent of the people in the Soviet Union voted to maintain the country in a referendum taken as part of the March 1991 election.

That result did not interest the pro-capitalist "democrats" in the least. In December 1991, the leaders began the process that would see the USSR dissolved within the next year.

It was leaders from within the summits of the Communist Party of the Soviet Union that led the offensive to destroy the Communist Party and dismantle the Soviet Union. This initiated the sale and looting of publicly owned factories, real estate, oil, gas and mining enterprises; and collectively owned agricultural lands and farms.

The wealth of society—at least significant parts of it—was turned over to a new class of private capitalists who soon became notorious for their opulence, decadence and theft. The legal social status of the working class was diminished and the standard of living of almost all workers plummeted.

The loss of factory jobs and access to medical care coupled with the attendant social problems and demoralization led to disastrous consequences. For example, a March 11, 1998, article in the Journal of the American Medical Association reported a drop in life expectancy for Soviet males from 63.8 years in 1990 to 57.7 years in 1994. The population in Russia actually dropped by over 500,000 people in the first eight months of 2000—the steepest drop ever during peacetime.

All the while, U.S. propaganda proclaimed that democracy and freedom had come at last to Russia.

A REVOLUTION LIKE NO OTHER

The Russian Revolution marked the first time in human history that the working classes, those without property, took the reins of power and held them. All previous revolutions in human history had transferred social and political power from one class of elite property owners to another.

The great French Revolution of 1789-93, for instance, had destroyed the power of the monarchy, feudal lords, landed nobility and aristocracy. The working classes had been the vanguard fighters in that revolution. But that revolution led to the French bourgeoisie taking power. The feudal mechanisms of exploitation based on serfdom were uprooted and destroyed, but were replaced by a new system of exploitation based on wage labor or wage slavery.

The October 1917 insurrection was altogether different from earlier revolutions. The social aims of the revolution, led by workers and poor farmers or peasants, were explicit about their class content.

Earlier revolutions masked their class character with broad slogans of freedom and equality "for all." The Russian Revolution, by contrast, explicitly proclaimed that eliminating all exploitation of the laboring classes was its principal objective on the road to achieving a society without classes. Operating under the Marxist conception that society was divided into antagonistic classes driven by mutual and irreconcilable differences, the explicit goal of the revolution was to achieve the political and social supremacy of the working classes over their former exploiters.

The banal slogan of "liberty and justice for all" was considered a mask concealing the true picture that the rich and privileged owners of private property had dominated society.

A WORKERS' CONSTITUTION

The victory of the Russian Revolution was based on the soviets—workers' councils that were the basic fighting organizations of the Russian workers. After the revolution, the soviets became the basic units of government. The first constitution adopted by the Congress of Soviets on July 10, 1918, set out the "fundamental goal" as "suppressing all human exploitation, abolishing forever the division of society into classes, ruthlessly suppressing all exploiters, bringing about the socialist organization of society and the triumph of socialism in all countries."[1]

None of the victorious revolutionary bourgeois governments from earlier epochs, even in their most revolutionary phases, would have thought of declaring this "fundamental goal" in their constitutions.

"As a first step toward the complete transfer of factories, works, shops, mines, railways and other means of production and of transport to the ownership of the workers' and peasants' Soviet Republic and to insure the supremacy of the laboring masses over the exploiters, the Congress ratifies the Soviet law on workers control of industry," reads another key provision in the constitution.[2]

Anticipating that the resistance of the overthrown exploiters would be greater following the revolution and that they would be aided by the imperialist governments of the world, the constitution declared that, "In order to secure the supremacy of the laboring masses and to guard against any possibility of the restoration of the power of the exploiters, the Congress declares the arming of the laboring population."[3]

This clause might have seemed to be written by people with a crystal ball. Within months after the 1918 Constitution was adopted, the country was plunged into a bloody civil war pitting class against class. Fourteen imperialist armies, including the United States, invaded Russia between 1918 and 1920. Three million people died.

And yet, to the amazement of all, the new workers' state survived the onslaught.

PROBLEMS OF SOCIALIST DEVELOPMENT

A huge part of the politicized and consciously communist working class of Russia died as volunteers fighting for the new social order, however. By the close of the civil war, the cities were decimated by hunger and disease. The factories were without raw materials. The urban proletariat started to return to the countryside in search of food.

The economy had contracted by nearly 90 percent compared to the 1914 pre-World War I level. In order to resume production,

Lenin and the Russian communists retreated in 1921 and allowed the return of capitalism and capitalists—but under the "supervision" of the Soviet state. The New Economic Policy was presented as an emergency step away from the communists' goals—to bend so as not to break. While it did stimulate production in both the countryside and the cities, it also led to a re-polarization of social classes, especially in the countryside.

It was not until 1928, when the economy was getting back on its feet, that the Soviet government resumed the push toward rapid socialization in the factories and the countryside.

In spite of these difficulties—all amid severe economic sanctions and blockade by the imperialists—the Soviet Union grew into the second largest economy in the world. Old, backward Russia entered the modern world using socialist methods of public ownership and central economic planning. It went from semi-feudalism in 1917 to a position where it launched the space age, putting the first spacecraft into orbit in 1957.

The Soviet people were among the most educated and cultured in the world. They accomplished in decades what had taken centuries to achieve in capitalist Europe.

For the most underdeveloped Soviet Republics in Central Asia and the Caucuses, the rate of economic and social development was even greater than that of Russia, although they still lagged behind. The Soviet Union's policies of prioritizing economic and social development in those regions were in effect the largest affirmative-action program in history.

In 1940, Hitler tried to re-impose capitalism in the Soviet Union by military force. Twenty-seven million Soviets died repelling and defeating fascism and liberating eastern and central Europe from the yoke of Nazi occupation. The Soviets never had a moment of reprieve following that awful carnage that devoured not only lives but the Soviet economic achievements of an entire post-revolutionary generation.

The Cold War with the United States—which began even before World War II had ended—required a massive diversion of funds from the civilian economy to the Soviet military. Despite these setbacks and non-stop drain on resources, the Soviet economy grew quickly using socialist methods.

BEHIND GORBACHEV'S RETREAT

The eventual overthrow of the Soviet Union was not caused by economic catastrophe. The growth rate in the economy had indeed slowed by the late 1970s. The high-tech revolution that led to an across-the-board restructuring of the industrial societies in Western Europe and the United States did in fact highlight a structural problem unique to the Soviet economic system.

The widespread transfer of the newest technologies in computers and electronics into industrial production in the western capitalist powers allowed for a major contraction of the work force. Millions of industrial workers in capitalist societies lost their jobs.

In the Soviet Union, a job was a right and the government was not legally entitled to deprive workers of employment. A careful process of job training and re-location for all workers whose jobs had become redundant slowed the pace of the introduction of the new technologies. Neither Margaret Thatcher and Ronald Reagan, nor the captains of industry, experienced these inhibitions.

This structural issue came on top of the enduring problem caused by the anti-communist economic blockade that prevented any transfer to the Soviet Union of technology that was revolutionizing the means of production in the advanced capitalist societies.

Gorbachev's economic reforms known as "perestroika" were intended to use market competition as a way to end or radically diminish the Soviet government's obligations to the working class. Market forces, rather than the enshrined legal rights of the working class, would determine employment patterns.

This section of the Soviet bureaucracy represented by Gorbachev identified socialist property relations and the Soviet Union's isolation from the locomotive of the world economy as the central obstacles impeding the country from sharing in the fruits of the revolution in technology that was sweeping the world in the last quarter of the 20th century.

Gorbachev and the Soviet reformers were convinced that only by ending the Cold War and liquidating centralized economic planning would U.S. imperialism accept the Soviet Union's entry into the rapidly accelerating model of a global economy.

Instead, the reforms set forces into motion inside and outside of the Soviet Communist Party who were completely bourgeois and pro-imperialist in their orientation. The pre-existing Soviet political system had driven them underground or into the Communist Party itself.

This relatively narrow stratum, as it struggled to de-legitimize and end Soviet power, did not promise the workers that they were about to loot their factories and society's wealth. They carried out the destruction of the existing government instead with a promise of ending corruption and bureaucratic abuse and bringing an end to the Cold War, which in turn would allow the people to enjoy the fruits of the world economy.

The 1917 Russian Revolution transformed private capitalist property into public property. That raised the possibility for the transition to socialism—but it hardly settled the question. It is evident by the overthrow of the socialist government that classes and class struggle do not disappear but take new forms during the post-capitalist period.

Pro-capitalist propaganda paints the high point of the 20th century as the "end of communism." Partisans of the working class and those who yearn for genuine equality will remember the Soviet Union not as the end of communism but as its first grand, real-life experiment. Its strengths and weaknesses will be assessed and incorporated by all future generations as invaluable lessons in the struggle to replace capitalist brutality, unemployment and poverty with a rational system that organizes and distributes the bounty of the world economy to meet the needs of human beings. □

Endnotes
1. 1918 Constitution of the Russian Socialist Federated Soviet Republic, Chapter 2, Article 3.
2. 1918 Constitution, Chapter 2, Article 3, point c.
3. 1918 Constitution, Chapter 2, Article 3, point g.

BURNING ISSUES:
WHY SOCIALISM?

The absurdity of capitalist overproduction

A glut of homes in a sea of homelessness

E **VERY** year in the United States, 3.5 million people experience a period of homelessness, nearly half of them children, according to a 2007 report by the National Law Center on Homelessness and Poverty.[1]

During the same period, 17.4 million houses stand vacant.[2] Another 2 million homeowners with subprime mortgages—over half of them African Americans—are expected to lose their homes to repossession in 2008.

The situation is absurd: Homes sitting vacant while children sleep in shelters or in the streets.

It does not end there. The housing crisis, the foreclosure epidemic, and the collapse of subprime mortgages have already begun to wreak havoc throughout the broader economy. There have been tens of thousands of layoffs in housing-related industries—construction, finance and real estate. Banks worldwide have tightened up their credit flows, especially to working class families. As workers feel the pinch, consumer spending will surely decline and the downturn will ripple through other areas of the economy.

Economists who were optimistically referring to this as a needed "correction" are now openly discussing the dreaded R-word, "recession." "According to our analysis, this [recession] isn't even forecast anymore but is a present day reality," chief North American economist at Merrill Lynch David Rosenberg told London's Daily Telegraph on Jan. 8.

Likewise, Nouriel Roubini, economist at the Stern School of Business at New York University, told the New York Times on Jan. 13, that the U.S. economy was at "risk of a systemic financial crisis."

CAPITALIST OVERPRODUCTION

How does the richest country in the world, employing an army of economists in think tanks, universities and government departments, find itself at the brink of an inescapable economic downturn that will throw millions out of their jobs and onto the street? Why did these financial geniuses with PhDs and MBAs not see where the economy was headed, and steer it in another direction?

Capitalism is an economic system that operates with one purpose: profits for individuals and corporations. This overarching logic determines how the capitalist owners and their administrators act and think. It also creates inescapable contradictions in the structure of the economy.

In the search for ever-higher profit margins and in competition with each other for greater market share, the capitalists produce far more of a given commodity than can be sold at the same rate of profit. The companies start to lower prices, hoping to sell the commodities they have produced—but there are no more buyers to be found. Investors pull out their capital, and the companies lay off workers and cut down operations in order to save their rate of profit.

This wasteful phenomenon of overproduction occurs on a small scale all the time, leading to layoffs and factory shutdowns. But periodically—when enough capital is wrapped up in the plummeting industry or industries—it leads to generalized economic recession or depression. This is called a crisis of overproduction.

That is what is driving the current housing crisis.

It is a phenomenon unique to capitalism. In previous social systems, economic crises were produced by national calamities—floods, droughts, hurricanes, earthquakes—leading to extended periods of food scarcity and starvation. Under capitalism, such economic crises emerge not because society has produced too little but because it has produced "too much." That does not mean too much in terms of meeting human needs, but too much to be sold at a profit.

CAN'T STOP, WON'T STOP

Under capitalism, workers are paid less than the value of the goods or services that they produce. The capitalist who employs the worker takes the remaining value—what socialist economists call surplus value, the basis for profit.

At the same time, each capitalist competes with other capitalists in order to return the highest rate of profit. To increase their rate of profit, capitalists try to find ways to cut the costs of production, through technological advances that can replace workers, cuts in wages and benefits, and outsourcing to lower-wage areas or countries.

In the short term, this leads to an immense return for the leading capitalists and individual investors. But over time the competing capitalists—if they are to survive—find ways to replicate those technological advances, and the overall rate of profit again stabilizes or sinks even lower.

As the capitalist accumulates profit, the quest immediately begins to find new investments that can return the same high rate of profit previously enjoyed. Capitalists normally do not just let their money sit, no matter how much they have. Their investors require them to keep making profits.

In the late 1990s, as economic crisis swept across East Asia and later South America, investors worldwide started to invest heavily in U.S. corporations and banks, which appeared more stable. The banks and corporations could not just let this money sit idle.

THE 'SUBPRIME' CRISIS

How could the banks turn all that newly acquired capital into greater gains? They began to lower interest rates on mortgages, allowing more working-class families to purchase new homes on credit. This policy was in effect a huge cash advance to the construction and banking industries—with the working class shouldering the risk.

Immediately, the construction industry began producing new homes and condominiums. Working class families were lured into purchasing homes at prices beyond what they could hope to pay on their constant or falling wages. At the same time, capitalists began purchasing homes and then immediately "flipping them"—reselling them at a higher price. Since the banks seemed to be a constant source of cheap credit, the new houses became more lavish and more expensive.

But the real-estate speculators built and purchased new houses without concern for the real needs and means of the buyers. In mid 2006, housing prices began to fall. Reports started surfacing about a spreading epidemic of foreclosures, as families defaulted on their loans. Many had been duped into accepting mortgages with enticing "teaser" rates that after a few years "reset" to higher rates that were completely unaffordable.

In the summer of 2007, it became clear that virtually the entire banking system had massively invested in the housing boom. Afraid they would not be getting back the money they had lent out, banks tightened up their credit and the entire economy teetered on the brink of disaster.

Now, millions of homes sit vacant in the United States—the most on record. "There are more ownerless houses in the United States today as a percentage of total inventory than at any time since records have been kept," wrote MSN Money's Jon Markman on Oct. 4, 2007.[3]

"For sale" signs swing haplessly in the wind and real-estate agents organize open houses that nobody attends. The homes are too expensive for working class families, especially because credit is now harder to come by and it is ever harder to sell existing homes. The upper strata of society, the ruling class, is numerically too small

Capitalist economy breeds a reserve army of unemployed.

PHOTO: FRANCES M. ROBERTS

to buy up and use all the condominiums and vacation homes that were built.

Residential construction has almost ground to a halt and industries related to construction materials are now in grave danger. Many real-estate companies have filed for bankruptcy and thousands of workers are out of their jobs.

Despite the absurdity of the situation, it is hard to imagine a different outcome. The high rate of profit necessitated it. If one of the real-estate companies had instead invested in affordable, low-income housing, it would have lost all its investors to the competitors who promised higher rates of return. If one of the banks had shifted its money out of the housing market altogether, another bank would have taken its place.

Nor could the capitalists have coordinated with one another to prevent the overproduction of housing. To coordinate in such a way would destroy the individual capitalist's competitive edge. It runs counter to the speculative instincts of a system based on competition.

The economic crisis was not caused by the bad decision-making of families, who were prodded at every turn to buy into the "American dream." Nor is it simply the product of predatory lenders. Both of these explanations put the onus on wrong-doing individuals. The scale of the foreclosure phenomenon shows that it comes from neither ignorance nor malice but from the very structure of the economy.

CAN RECESSIONS BE ELIMINATED UNDER CAPITALISM?

Generalized crises of overproduction have occurred roughly once per decade in the United States for the last 150 years. The current economic crisis, a product of overproduction and the over-accumulation of capital, is an inevitable outcome of the logic of the economic system.

Some capitalist economists have tried to come to grips with the fact that the "free market" cannot solve its own contradictions. Followers of economist John Maynard Keynes, in particular, claim that the government can avert or minimize capitalist crisis by taking a more active role in controlling the money supply through the Federal Reserve, giving out money to promote consumer spending and reassure investors.

"Free market" rhetoric aside, federal intervention in the economy is now routine. While there has not been a downturn on the scale of the Great Depression of the 1930s, this routine intervention has not been able to stop periodic recessions. It cannot solve the fundamental contradictions of the economy.

Today's recession is out of the Federal Reserve's control. "Whatever [the Federal Reserve is] going to do," Stern School economist Roubini admitted, "it's going to be cosmetic." (New York Times, Jan. 13, 2008)

The crisis is not the product of bad luck or poor planning. We are not faced with recession because a big-shot economist forgot one decimal point in his formulas, because some investment banker's computer froze, or because the chairman of the Federal Reserve uttered the wrong phrase in his report.

We are faced with crisis because the capitalist economy has a fundamental contradiction. Although the production and reproduction of the economy draws in millions of workers, who consciously or not work together, the fruits of the economy are owned by a tiny minority who compete with one another based on profit. Enormous technological advances are wasted because the economy as a whole is unplanned, anarchic and thus prone to disaster.

ANOTHER WAY

It does not have to be this way.

Socialism is a different economic system operating according to a different logic. It functions according to a conscious plan, measuring the productive capacity of all of society with social needs.

Instead of being absorbed by individual capitalists and invested according to the needed rate of profit, surplus value—the social product created by the workers—is reinvested into the country's infrastructure, into technology, and into cultural and recreational developments. There is no such thing as an inherent tendency toward overaccumulation or overproduction under socialism.

The current housing crisis could not possibly have taken place if the United States were a socialist country.

This is not wishful or utopian thinking. There are now decades of experience, positive and negative, in socialist planning and construction.

In its 74 years of existence, the Soviet Union never experienced a general crisis of overproduction. Although it developed into the second most powerful industrial economy on the planet, it never experienced the boom-bust cycle of the industrialized capitalist countries.

Even when its rate of growth slowed in the 1970s, it never went through negative growth that characterizes recessions under capitalism.

The same is true for China, despite the massive inroads that capitalist production have made since the late 1970s.

The goal of socialists is to get rid of the contradiction between socially created wealth and private accumulation and ownership. The wealth of society is produced collectively, so it should be owned and managed collectively.

The economic crises serve as periodic reminders that capitalism is condemned to die sooner or later. But it will not self-destruct. A revolutionary movement must bring about its demise. □

Endnotes

1. National Coalition for the Homeless, Fact Sheet 2, August 2007, www.nationalhomeless.org/publications/facts/How_Many.pdf.
2. Jon Markman, comment on "For home builders, the worst is yet to come," www.msn.com, comment posted on October 4, 2007, http://articles.moneycentral.msn.com/Investing/SuperModels/For HomeBuildersTheWorstIsToCome.aspx?page = all.
3. Ibid.

Rehabilitation will only be a priority under socialism

Dismantle the racist prison system!

THE United States has the largest prison population in the world. According to a Bureau of Statistics report, over 2.2 million people are in U.S. prisons. With another 5 million people in "the system," over 7 million people are either on parole, probation or incarcerated.

The United States also has the largest prison population relative to its total population: 750 per 100,000 people were in prison in 2006, according to statistics cited by the International Centre for Prison Studies at King's College in Britain on June 21, 2006. This number would be even higher if immigrant detention centers and military jails were included.

For 35 consecutive years the U.S. prison population soared. Until the mid 1970s, the U.S. prison population ranged from 200,000 to 215,000. In the 1980s, the numbers doubled. They doubled again in the early 1990s.

According to an Aug. 29, 2007, Bureau of Justice Statistics report, the amount of money spent on prisons went from $9 billion in 1982 to $65 billion in 2005.

PRISONS IN THE UNITED STATES

The prison system magnifies all the contradictions of capitalist society.

For example, the day-to-day reality of racism for African Americans in the United States is on extreme display in the U.S. prison system. Approximately 1 million African American men under the age of 40 are behind bars—nearly half the entire prison population. Twelve percent of African American men ages 20 to 34 were in prison in 2003, compared with 1.6 percent of white men in the same age group.[1]

Black males are incarcerated at more than six times the rate of white males. In seven states, the rate is more than 10 times the rate of whites. In 2004, Hawaii had the lowest incarceration rate of Blacks, 851 per 100,000—a rate that is still higher than the state with the highest incarceration rate of whites, Oklahoma at 740 per 100,000.[2] A report issued in January 2004 by the Sentencing Project entitled "Schools and Prisons," estimates that one out of every eight Black men between the ages of 25 and 29 are incarcerated on any given day.

There is no evidence that the increased rate of incarceration has had any impact on lowering crimes rates.

Latinos are incarcerated at double the rate of whites. This rate would be higher if the detention centers for undocumented immigrants were included. Entire families can be kept in these detention centers for any length of time without notifying anyone. Prisoners are held in small cells, receiving barely enough to eat and very limited medical attention.

An April 19, 2007 report by the Women's Prison Association reported that more than 200,000 women are in prison. The rate of women being incarcerated is increasing at nearly double that of men. Women from oppressed communities are impacted even more. The incarceration rate for Latina women is double that of white women. Black women are incarcerated at five times the rate of white women.

Prisons are becoming more overcrowded by the day. According to the previously cited International Centre for Prison Studies report, U.S. prisons have an overall occupancy level of 106.9 percent. Overcrowding has been at the root of many prison rebellions, like the April 24, 2007, uprising by almost 500 inmates in an Indiana prison protesting living conditions.

PRISONS AND CRIME

The official justification for imprisoning more people is to bring down the crime rate. But there is no evidence that the increased jailing rate has had any impact on lowering crimes rates.

The U.S. prison rate began to skyrocket in 1975, according to data presented in a 2003 report by the Prison Policy Initiative. Crime rates, however, did not fall for nearly 25 years. In fact, the crime index rate rose steadily from 1976 to 1992, from 467.8 to 757.5 per 100,000.

A decline in violent offenses did not start until 1993—corresponding to a fall in unemployment and a drop in the percentage of males in the "high-risk" 15- to 24-year-old age group. Violent crime rates dropped in Canada the same year with no corresponding increase in the number of prisons or prisoners.

The trend in crime rates is related more to the ups and downs of the capitalist economy than how many people are put behind bars.

According to a report issued by the Sentencing Project in December 2006, over half of federal prison cases were drug convictions. Only 11 percent are for violent crimes. The severe sentences for drug charges have affected women at an alarming rate.

Between 1988 and 1994, the number of drug-related incarcerations rose 156 percent. Although whites and African Americans have a similar history of drug use, 75 percent of those convicted for drug crimes are Black.

BEHIND THE SKYROCKETING PRISON POPULATION

The prison-industrial complex is a multi-million-dollar business. Prison workers make furniture, license plates, clothing and much more. In 2005, prisons produced $765 million worth of goods according to the July 13, 2007, Congressional Research Service report for Congress, "Federal Prison Industries." According to that report, prisoners are made to work for pennies, and 50 percent of prison wages are used to cover any costs accrued while on trial.

But these profits alone cannot explain the prison explosion—not in the trillion-dollar U.S. economy. So what is the underlying reason behind the expansion of U.S. prisons over the last 30 years?

The prison boom parallels the high-tech revolution and the massive restructuring of the U.S. economy beginning in the 1970s. The technological advances spurred on by the computerization of industries were being sold as ways to enrich both workers and the U.S. economy.

As advances in technology soared to new levels, workers jobs began to vanish. Industrial bosses made more products with fewer workers.

A Feb. 18, 2004, Congressional Budget Office report shows the dramatic impact of the de-industrialization. In 1979, there were close to 19.5 million manufacturing jobs in the United States. By 1983, that number had dropped to around 16.5 million. Hundreds of plants were shut down.

This trend has continued unabated. According to an August 2007 report by the U.S. Bureau of Labor Statistics, "Charting the U.S. Labor Market in 2006," close to 3 million manufacturing workers were laid off in the United States between 2001 and 2006, bringing manufacturing employment to just over 14 million.

Underemployment and unemployment continue to grow. Millions of workers now work in non-union low-paying jobs in the service industry. Record numbers of employees are still being hired. According to the BLS, in 2007 more than 85 percent of all non-farm jobs in the United States are in the service industry—116 million out of 138 million.

In December 2007, BLS figures report around 13.7 million workers in the United States were unemployed, underemployed or are "marginally attached," meaning they had stopped looking for work.

In these circumstances, prisons are used as a way to control and intimidate the population, especially poor communities. Prisons are the ruling class' solution to the contradiction of "surplus" workers in the high-tech era and the deepening capitalist economic crisis. Crucial to protecting the interests and private property of the capitalist class, prisons function as warehouses for unemployed and poor workers.

As an integral part of the capitalist state—prisons are tools of repression used by the ruling class to keep its position in society and exploit the working class.

SOCIALISM—THE WAY FORWARD

U.S. capitalism proves with each passing year that its solution to poverty and unemployment—especially for the African American and Latino communities—is prison. It has given new meaning to Lenin's description of czarist Russia as "a prison house of nations."

Among the very first steps in the socialist revolution in the United States would be the dismantling of the U.S. prison-industrial complex—what has become known as a "concentration camp for poor and working people." The millions who have been incarcerated for nonviolent and petty crimes would be released on the spot.

That is not to say that a socialist United States would be able to do without prisons entirely. Even in Russia, before the first socialist revolution, Lenin wrote in "State and Revolution," "During the transition from capitalism to communism, suppression is still necessary; but it is the suppression of the minority of exploiters—the counter-revolutionary capitalist property owners and their military agents—by the majority of the exploited."

Although the state is in essence an instrument of class suppression for a society's ruling class, it also has non-repressive functions as well. These functions would also need to be addressed under a new post-revolutionary social regime. Traffic police, for instance, would need to regulate and enforce the law.

A revolution in the United States would inherit working-class communities plagued by social alienation, drug addiction, anti-social behavior, and extreme sexism. A new revolutionary state would still be confronted, especially initially, with the need to protect and

Unemployment is inherent to capitalism.

PHOTO: BILL HACKWELL

defend working-class communities from crimes common in U.S. capitalist society.

It is obvious that the current U.S. prison system is bankrupt when it comes to addressing these problems. Murder rates are soaring in cities with high unemployment rates. Every four minutes another violent crime is carried out against a woman. Mass incarceration does not affect these problems.

The complex issues of individual and social crime can be solved under and only by socialism. Under a workers' state, punishment of individuals for criminal acts and extreme anti-social behavior would continue during a transitional phase—but with a huge difference. Punishment and removal of individuals from the overall community may be necessary, but it is not the answer to the social problem of individual crime. Guaranteed social and economic rights, empowering workers to control society, using the instruments of mass education to overcome racism and sexism—these are elements that will help society overcome anti-social behaviors.

The current prison system would be dismantled and replaced with a humane and effective set of institutions. Cuba's socialist revolution offers important lessons in what that might look like.

The International Centre for Prison Studies estimates that some 60,000 people are imprisoned in Cuba. Cuba is still dealing with all the contradictions of centuries of class rule and 250 years of predatory capitalism and imperialism. But what do Cuban prisons look like?

No prisoners are undernourished. The Cuban penal system offers job-training programs in nursing, physical education, basic hygiene, laboratory, ultrasound or X-ray technicians. The provision of libraries is also part of the program.

These programs were designed to "convert prisons into schools" and are part of what is known as "Task 500." Havana-based journalist Susan Hurlich detailed the project in a March 2004 essay called, "Inside Cuba's Prisons: Health Care and Vocational Training."

"Task 500" was started in 2000 with the aim of providing educational opportunities and a vocation to inmates. The long-term goal is social reintegration.

Prisoners who obtain a nursing degree, receive a diploma just like all nursing students in Cuba. Their diploma will not disclose where they studied. Once they are paroled or have completed their sentences, they can get jobs in community hospitals or continue to study for a bachelor's degree in nursing.

If the nursing graduates are still in prison, they can help staff the National Hospital for Prisoners. Inmates who work in prisons receive the same wages as someone working outside of prison, Hurlich reports.

In January, one of Cuba's best-known singers, Silvio Rodriguez, began a concert tour of 13 prisons. "There is a strong cultural movement in the prisons," he told Granma International.

Rodriguez and the Ministry of the Interior, which runs the prisons, sponsored the tour. It aims "to contribute to the rehabilitation of the prisoners and their reinsertion into society," according to a Jan. 14, AP report.

This kind of genuine rehabilitation can only take place in the context of a society based on human needs, not on the enrichment of a tiny few. It is only possible with socialism. □

Endnotes

1. New York Times, April 7, 2003.
2. The Sentencing Project, "Statistics by State," www.sentencingproject.org.

It will take a revolution

Eradicating the scourge of racism from U.S. society

N August 2006, an African American student in Jena, La., asked his school principal for permission to sit under what had been known as a "whites only" tree in the center of the school's courtyard. The following day, three nooses in the school's colors were found hanging from the tree.

School administrators tried to diffuse the situation by saying that the noose hangings were a prank directed at members of the school's rodeo team, but police were called in several times in the aftermath because of racially charged confrontations between Black and white students. The white students who hung the nooses were let off with three-day suspensions.

Jena is a small town in Louisiana with a population of 2,971, of which 85 percent is white. One out of eight students at Jena High School is Black.

On Dec. 1, 2006, 16-year-old Robert Bailey, a Black student at Jena High School, was invited to a barn party. When he arrived, white students refused to allow him in. A crowd outside the barn attacked and beat Bailey.

Three days later, Justin Baker—one of Bailey's attackers—publicly defended the white students who had hung the nooses a few months prior. In response, several Black students confronted Baker. A fight followed; Baker was taken to the hospital for minor injuries. He was released a few hours later to attend a ceremony at the school.

The Jena police arrested the six students who had confronted Baker. The students were expelled from Jena High School. Prosecutors charged five of the youth with attempted second-degree murder and conspiracy to commit murder, while a sixth was charged in juvenile court.

The case of the "Jena Six"—Robert Bailey, Theo Shaw, Carwin Jones, Bryant Purvis, Jesse Ray Beard and Mychal Bell—provoked mass marches and rallies across the country. On Sept. 20, 2007, tens of thousands poured into Jena to demand that the prosecutors drop the charges. The outpouring forced the prosecutors to drop the most serious criminal charges, although all still faced juvenile charges.

NOT JUST JENA

How is it that 145 years after the Emancipation Proclamation that ended slavery in the United States, African Americans are still subject to threats and violence if they do not "stay in their place?" How is it that 40 years after the civil rights movement smashed Jim Crow segregation in the South, there is still a racist judicial system specifically designed to railroad and corral young Black men in particular?

The case of the Jena Six struck such a chord with African Americans because their situation, and that of the small Black community in overwhelmingly white Jena, La., are typical of what African Americans experience every day in the United States. Racism is part of the fabric of U.S. society and is the biggest single obstacle to working-class unity and revolution in the United States.

> *Racism is part of the fabric of U.S. society, and is the biggest single obstacle to working-class unity and revolution in the United States.*

The Jena Six case is not really about a school brawl or aggravated battery. It is about whether racist prosecutors and courts can continue to enforce a reign of terror against Black communities. It is about whether racist terrorists can flout their symbol, the noose, with impunity. It is about whether African Americans will be able to push back the racists—and whether white workers and progressives from all nationalities will stand at their side in that fight.

After all, the noose embodies the violent, terrorizing legacy of slavery, lynchings and racism in the United States. To Black America and all descendants of slaves, a noose represents systematic political terrorism. Thousands of African Americans fell victim to lynching after the Civil War, during Reconstruction and the terror that followed, and during the civil rights movements of the 1950s and 1960s.

RACISM AND CAPITALISM

Living in the United States, it would be tempting to think that racism is part of human nature. Every ruling class tries to claim that its particular form of exploitation is "human nature."

In fact, history is filled with examples of Black people and people of African descent earning the respect of whites. The Roman general Lusius Quietus, described as a "man of Moorish race," was designated by the emperor Trajan as his successor before the emperor was killed in 117. In ancient Europe, the term "Moor" referred to anyone of African descent or with dark skin. A number of Roman emperors were Moors, including Septimius Severus (193-211).

In European Christian tradition, the Three Magi represent the great civilizations of the world. Throughout the Medieval era, Balthazar is generally depicted in paintings as a Black king.

However, with the emergence of the slave trade associated with the conquest of the Americas, that respect had to be shattered. How could millions of people be subjected to subhuman conditions, packed into ships like cargo, and abused in ways worse than animals, if they were human beings on an equal footing with all others?

Racism emerged as the ideological justification of slavery. For 350 years, it shaped the relations between Blacks and whites in the United States. Racism and slavery were the foundation of the development of capitalism in the United States and in Europe.

The combination of slavery with the dynamics of capitalism and its quest for profit made the system of slavery in the Americas far more brutal than anything seen before in history. It was of a completely different nature than the slavery practiced in ancient Greece, in barbarian Europe or in pre-colonial Africa. This was oppression on a massive scale, accompanied by a brutality unparalleled in world history to that point.

Africans stolen and sold in the slave trade came from a very settled culture with strong communal relations and tribal customs. Once in United States, however, African slaves were subject to whites with guns, whips and courts to uphold their profit-driven brutality.

In North America, African slaves were stripped of their identity-language, dress, customs, family and spiritual practices. It was this isolation of African slaves that allowed American capitalism the competitive edge in imperialist conquest.

In his autobiography, "Narrative of the Life of Frederick Douglass," Douglass, a slave who taught himself to read and write, asked the question:

> Why am I a slave? Why are some people slaves, and others masters? Was there ever a time when this was not so? How did the relation commence? ... I was not very long in finding out the true solution of the matter. It was not color, but crime, not God, but man, that afforded the true explanation of the existence of slavery; nor was I long in finding out another important truth, viz: what man can make, man can unmake.

REBELLION AND REVOLUTION

The history of the United States cannot be told without the constant struggles of slaves for freedom and of African Americans for liberation after slavery was abolished in 1863. Hundreds of slave rebellions took place in the centuries leading up to the Civil War.

The Civil War was initiated by the slave-owning ruling class in the southern states after concluding that the 1860 election of Abraham Lincoln meant that their plans to dominate the entire United States were failing. Confronted with this reality, they seceded from the union to form a new country based entirely on slave-owning production in an agriculturally dominant economy.

The northern industrial capitalists, in need of a flexible labor pool that could expand or contract according to the needs of the capitalist market, depended on "free labor" as opposed to slave labor. Deriving their profits from hired wage labor, the northern capitalists considered the southern system to be an impediment to the expansion of capitalism in North America. Their opposition to the slave owners had nothing to do with a principled opposition to a social system that justified its existence based on white supremacy.

But in the course of waging that war, the northern capitalists were driven by the imperative needs to secure a military victory to emancipate the slaves—and, in turn, unleash the revolutionary social force of an armed African American population. That became a major factor in breaking the back of the Confederacy. It also laid the basis for the demands of racial and social equality after the war.

Between 1865 and 1877, Reconstruction governments grew up in the South. The former slave owners and secessionists were barred from participating in the political process. The northern army occupied the South and imposed a military dictatorship allowing for the first blossoming of democracy for freed slaves who formed coalitions with poor whites.

The Reconstruction period ebbed as the northern capitalists and their political operatives in the Republican Party defeated the

Multinational unity is key in the struggle against racism.

radical abolitionists inside the party and in Congress. The Ku Klux Klan unleashed a wave of terror throughout the South. Lynchings by the hooded thugs of the defeated slavocracy became the symbol of counterrevolution and a historic defeat of the bourgeois-democratic revolution in the South. The KKK victory became secure when the federal government agreed to remove all northern troops from the South in 1877.

The result was a de facto alliance between the victorious capitalist class and the old slavocracy to force the newly emancipated Black population into subordination through Klan terror and a century of apartheid, which became known as Jim Crow segregation. This apartheid system was not just in the South. The U.S. armed forces, drawing units from all over the country, only desegregated in 1948.

The noose was the principal symbol of the state-sponsored or permitted terrorism against a whole people.

It would take the mass civil rights movement and the Black liberation struggle of the 1950s and 1960s to formally end legal apartheid and official white supremacy.

Yet to this day, police departments in cities across the country, from New York to Los Angeles, patrol Black and Latino communities as an occupying army. Courts in cities and towns alike have in effect two justice systems: one for whites and one for Black and Latino people. Every statistic of social well-being shows the impact of racism on the African American nation.

Racism is firmly entrenched in the system of capitalist exploitation. Eliminating one will require eliminating the other.

WHAT DIFFERENCE DOES A REVOLUTION MAKE?

Cuba, too, experienced the enslavement of Africans under Spanish colonialism. It, too, was plagued by institutionalized racism and inequality for centuries. Afro-Cubans had the highest unemployment and poverty rates.

After the 1959 Cuban Revolution, Cuban leader Fidel Castro delivered a proclamation against racism, declaring, "We shouldn't have to pass a law to establish a right that should belong to every human being and member of society. ... Nobody can consider themselves to be of pure race, much less a superior race. Virtue, personal merit, heroism, generosity, should be the measure of people, not skin color."

This proclamation was backed by new revolutionary laws and courts. The new constitution outlawed racism and sexism, making them crimes punishable by law. Moreover, the constitution committed the state "to create all the conditions that will make the principle of equality real."

Revolutionary Cuba tied its fate to the people of the world struggling against racism and exploitation. It has sent troops dozens of times to struggles for national liberation in Africa. From its first expedition of soldiers, led by Ernesto Che Guevara, to aid the Congo after its independence from Belgium between 1960 and 1965, to its militant solidarity with the anti-apartheid movement in South Africa, Angola, and Namibia, Cuban internationalists have faced off against the forces of racism and imperialism. That support was recognized during Nelson Mandela's visit to the island in 1991, shortly after his release from an apartheid prison.

While Cuba defended national liberation abroad, it also advanced the Afro-Cuban population in Cuba. Before 1959, Afro-Cubans mostly lived in the poorest and most dilapidated housing in Cuba. Today, there are more Black-owned homes in Cuba than any country in the world, because rents were reduced post-revolution and tenants were later granted ownership.

When the African American actor, civil rights activist and communist Paul Robeson visited the Soviet Union in 1934, he found that the country was virtually free of racial prejudice. He stated, "Here, for the first time in my life I walk in full human dignity." That historic achievement was rolled back by the counterrevolution that ended the Soviet system in 1991, which unleashed a wave of racism, great-nation chauvinism and conflicts between the Soviet's vast myriad of nationalities and ethnic groups.

CHALLENGES FOR U.S. COMMUNISTS

Uprooting racism will not happen automatically by expropriating the capitalists' property. The centuries of super-oppression against the African American people and other oppressed nationalities will require special attention based on a Leninist understanding of the right of oppressed peoples to self-determination.

First and foremost, the legacy of slavery must be recognized and addressed. Harper's Magazine estimated a total of over $97 trillion owed for over 222,505,049 hours of unpaid forced labor between 1619 and 1865 at 6 percent interest. A socialist revolution in the United States would fulfill the essence of the promise made by the federal government to former slaves in 1865 of "40 acres and a mule." That promise of reparations was immediately repealed by Andrew Johnson who assumed the presidency after Lincoln was assassinated.

Providing real reparations to the African American people based on the expropriated wealth of the super-rich bankers who profited from the system of slavery would be among the first acts of a socialist government in the United States.

Racism and hate crimes, like that which took place in Jena, would be punishable crimes. A massive education campaign would address white workers, emphasizing the need for solidarity, internationalism and working-class unity.

African Americans and other oppressed nationalities would be guaranteed representation at every level of the new revolutionary government. The model of the Soviet Union's Council of Nationalities provides a useful example of how to increase and equalize power for oppressed nations inside of a multi-national state.

Many more measures would be implemented as millions of African Americans enter the revolutionary movement with the energy and creativity that they have contributed to so many movements in the past.

The main obstacle to these measures is the capitalist class, which benefits from the social stratification and division of workers by race and gender. Bosses will always exploit social inequalities and special oppression to divide the working class and get higher profits from these disenfranchised communities.

That is why none of these measures can be carried out except in the struggle to eliminate capitalism. □

Can sexism be eliminated under capitalism?

H **OW** can women be liberated from the many bonds of sexism in U.S. society? For well over a century, powerful women leaders and mass movements have struggled to accomplish that challenge.

Yet the situation remains grim. Despite the fanfare of high-profile women candidates during election season, the reality for millions of women is not pretty: threats of violence and harassment, discrimination on the job, and the drudgery of sole responsibility for housework and child care.

Every two minutes in the United States, a woman is sexually assaulted, while every six minutes one is raped. That amounts to about 200,000 women victims every year.

Thirty-one percent of U.S. women have been physically or sexually abused by an intimate partner at some point in their lives. A woman is battered by an intimate partner every 15 seconds. One-third of female murder victims are killed by an intimate partner.

Sexism means more profits for the capitalist class of owners and bosses. On average, a woman in the United States is paid about 75 cents for every dollar that a man earns for the same work.

The lack of maternity leave, child care and health care falls hardest on women workers. For most of the 10 million single mothers in the United States, for example, adequate day care is a huge expense. Average childcare costs range from $4,000 to $10,000 per year. The Census Bureau found that families with less that $14,000 annual income spend more than 25 percent of their income on child care.

While poor and working-class women might feel sexism most severely, it cuts across all income lines. The American Association of University Women Educational Foundation did a study of college-educated women. During college years, women have on average higher grades in every major. Yet one year out of college, women earned 80 percent of what men were earning for the same jobs. Ten years later, the gap had widened, with women were earning 69 percent of what men were earning.

Sexism is reinforced through every media in capitalist society. Women are depicted in the most degrading, humiliating and demeaning manner. For young women, the result can be psychologically and sometimes physically destructive.

Reproductive rights are under constant attack. Even though abortion is still legal, new regulations are being imposed every year. In 2003, close to 90 percent of all U.S. counties had no abortion provider; in non-metropolitan areas, the figure reached 97 percent.

The picture is grim. It would have been far worse without the mass movements for women's rights—from the suffrage movement at the turn of the 20th century to the mass women's liberation movement that arose in the 1960s and 1970s. These struggles led to real gains, including winning the right to vote and forcing the U.S. Supreme Court to acknowledge a woman's right to privacy and to control her body with the 1973 *Roe v. Wade* decision, as well as the winning of important reforms in the struggle against gender-based violence. But, as Frederick Douglass noted long ago, there is no progress without fierce and determined struggles.

ROOTED IN CAPITALISM—NOT HUMAN NATURE

It is common to hear that sexism and the oppression of women are part of the natural order of things. It has "always been this way," we are told. Conservative pundits frequently cry out for a return to "traditional" family order. Even some militant supporters of women's liberation claim that women have always been oppressed throughout the ages.

History tells a different story entirely. Numerous anthropologists like Eleanor Burke Leacock and Karen Sacks have shown that for most of human history, women's status as second-class citizens did not exist. For the vast majority of history, class society and exploitation did not exist. People lived in a primitive communal or classless society. The family bloodline was traced through the mother's line, which anthropologists call "mother right." All material wealth was owned and distributed communally.

Reproductive rights—a basic right for women—are under constant attack under capitalism.

PHOTO: BILL HACKWELL

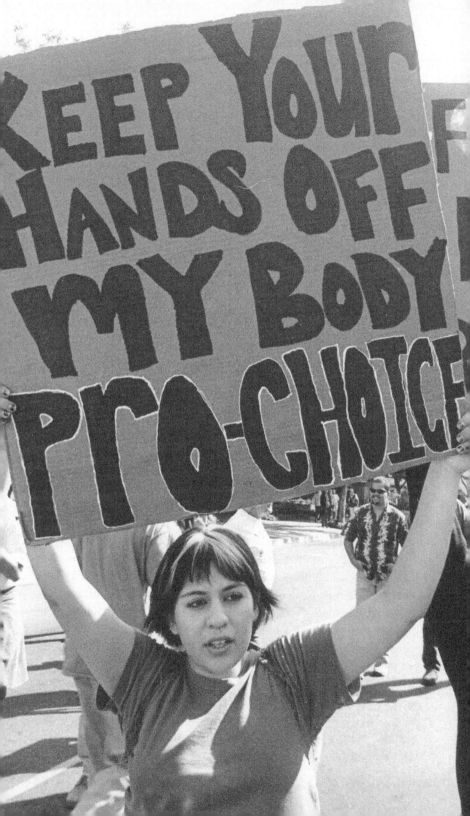

Women's oppression can be traced to the "world historic defeat" of the female sex, in the words of 19th-century German communist Friedrich Engels, when in the transition to class exploitation, women became the property of men.

Since that time, women's oppression has been a fundamental prop of class exploitation. The form has changed, but the essence has been remarkably universal and similar since the first advent of class society that began in some areas thousands of years ago. In the area that is now the United States, this change occurred dynamically within the last 500 years, coinciding with the large-scale emigration from Europe's class society and the subsequent genocide against Native society, which had until then largely retained non-class and communal forms.

Under U.S. monopoly capitalism, sexism means the ability to earn super-profits from a lower-paid sector of the workforce. It also divides the working class, pitting men against women and trapping some male workers into identifying with their male boss instead of their women coworkers on the basis of common class interests.

In other words, sexism is in the interest of the U.S. ruling class.

That means that the way to eradicate sexism is to remove the ruling class from power and dismantle its system of exploitation and its right to private profit. The path to true women's liberation is part and parcel of the fight for socialism.

SOCIALISM AND WOMEN'S LIBERATION

History's greatest examples of the emancipation of women as full and equal actors in society and the opportunity to live to their fullest potential have come following socialist revolutions. Following the 1917 Russian Revolution, for example, women gained rights that they had not yet won in the most advanced capitalist countries: the right to vote and the right to abortion on demand. Restrictions on divorce were removed. The Bolsheviks abolished laws that enforced gender inequality and threw out anti-gay laws. Women were granted economic and social rights in the constitution. Many of these advances were eviscerated in the 1930s during a period of conservative retrenchment following the revolution. During and following World War II, the political status and social rights of Soviet women made a new round of gains.

After the 1949 Chinese Revolution, women's associations were formed in rural villages to combat the strict subjugation of women, and a mass campaign targeting women's illiteracy was launched.

In Cuba, the Federation of Cuban Women was formed a year after the 1959 revolution to address women's issues. It helped to establish child care, paid maternity leave, free medical care and expanded educational opportunities, and made it possible for women to enter every area of the workforce.

In 1975, the Federation was instrumental in shaping the Family Code in Cuba. This code made it the legal obligation of men to share in the housework and child-rearing responsibilities. There have been countrywide discussions of the Family Code through congresses, educational materials and the mass media. Although a constitutional law on housework does not by itself eliminate sexist patterns, it was an important statement and tool in advancing women's formal rights.

Today, women in Cuba make up 66.4 percent of all technicians, mid-level professionals and higher-degree professionals. They make up 72 percent of all education workers, 67 percent of health workers, and 43 percent of all science workers. These figures demonstrate women's independence and contribution to the economic development of the country.

Women's representation in government positions is one of the highest in the world. Cuban women hold 47 percent of the Supreme Court and 49 percent of judgeships, comprise 60 percent of public prosecutors and hold 36 percent of the seats in Cuba's National Assembly.

Cuba has over 1,000 child care facilities on the island of 11.4 million. Daycare centers have on-site doctors and nurses. Eye, ear and dental exams are done free at the centers. Women had the right to one year of maternity leave, six months paid and another six months unpaid leave. In 2003, paid parental leave was extended to one full year for mothers or fathers.

The Cuban people have been able to do so much toward the liberation of women only because the working class smashed the capitalist state and began the reconstruction of society on a socialist basis.

Socialist revolution does not liberate women overnight. But the socialist organization of society lays the foundation for liberating women from the economic slavery they are subjected to in class society. In this way only socialism offers the complete road to liberation for women. □

Insuring the rights won by the LGBT movement

D **ESPITE** the period of political reaction in the United States started in the 1980s, the lesbian-gay-bi-transgendered movement has achieved significant gains in winning some measure of equality and dignity for sexual and gender minorities. In the almost 40 years since the 1969 Stonewall Rebellion, 20 states, the District of Columbia and over 140 municipalities and counties have enacted anti-discrimination ordinances.

Forty-five states and Washington, D.C. have statutes criminalizing various types of anti-LGBT hate-motivated violence or intimidation. In 2003, the Supreme Court issued the *Lawrence vs. Texas* decision, rendering anti-LGBT sodomy laws unconstitutional. This ended the long history of legal criminalization of lesbian and gay sex.

There has even been progress toward the once unimaginable demand for same-sex marriage rights. Massachusetts became the first state to enact marriage equality in 2004. Five states—Connecticut, Vermont, New Jersey, California and New Hampshire—recognize civil unions with almost all the rights of marriage. Four more states— Maine, Hawaii, Oregon and Washington—along with Washington, D.C., recognize some rights for same-sex couples.

Given this seemingly steady progress under capitalist democracy, is the struggle for socialism really relevant for LGBT people?

CAPITALISM MEANS CONSTANT STRUGGLE

It would be a mistake to conclude from the gains made so far that progress for the LGBT community is inevitable. On the contrary, it is a basic lesson for all oppressed and exploited people that under class society no gains come without constant struggle.

An example is the AIDS crisis that broke out in the early 1980s. AIDS was first identified as a new illness affecting mostly gay men. It was originally called GRID, Gay Related Immune Deficiency. The humanitarian crisis was accompanied by a political crisis.

Right-wing preachers and other anti-gay bigots whipped up a climate of near hysteria against gay people and all people with AIDS. The immediate need for medical care and research had to be fought for amid a larger battle against discrimination and bigotry.

A tremendous and powerful movement arose. Thousands of LGBT people and their allies, including many people afflicted with AIDS, marched, demonstrated and participated in civil disobedience actions. In addition to right-wing politicians and reactionary religious bigots, the movement targeted the healthcare system, winning much-needed medical care and services.

These struggles radicalized a whole generation of young LGBT people. They were largely responsible for many of the advances the LGBT movement has made in the reactionary period since.

Progress under capitalism is impossible without struggle. Gains that have been fought for and won can be taken away with

Under capitalism, every social gain for LGBT people is under attack. Here, supporters of same-sex marriage, San Francisco, May 17, 2004

PHOTO: BILL HACKWELL

the stroke of a pen. While 10 states recognize some form of same sex marriage rights 26 states have constitutional amendments banning gay marriage.

ANTI-LGBT OPPRESSION ROOTED IN CLASS SOCIETY

Marxists see the root of gender and sexual oppression as being important to the emergence of class society and the corresponding emergence of patriarchy. In pre-class society, men and women were on equal terms, children were everyone's responsibility and sexuality was unconstrained. There is now a wealth of anthropological evidence for this on every continent.

As class society evolved, the transmission of wealth and property from one generation to the next becomes a primary concern for the property-owning class. Society's institutions were designed to enforce and protect this accumulation of property. Since motherhood is far easier to establish—and to control—than fatherhood, extensive restrictions on female sexuality were imposed. Anyone who challenged these restrictions, including those who did not conform to the male-dominated heterosexual norm, were repressed.

As LGBT activists have argued in recent years, the line between male and female genders is not always clear. It is not a simple biological matter as right-wing moralists claim. In pre-class society, it did not matter much if someone was not clearly a man or woman, or if someone's sexuality did not produce children. In patriarchal society, these issues matter a great deal.

Expressions that blur or bridge the divide between men and women threaten the deeply-ingrained social schism of class society. The basic social instinct of mutual support is disrupted by the need of the ruler to divide the ruled.

THE WAY FORWARD

It is for that reason that socialists see the ultimate answer to ending anti-LGBT oppression in the end of class society. Until that time, every step forward will have to come with tremendous struggle, and none of those steps will be secure.

That is not to say that a victorious socialist revolution will automatically guarantee equality. The 1917 socialist revolution in Russia initially eliminated the repressive anti-gay laws of the czarist regime.

However, after the death of Lenin, less revolutionary Soviet govern-ments reimposed many of those restrictions.

The 1959 Cuban revolution did not immediately address the problems of anti-gay oppression and bigotry. It took several decades for the revolutionary Cuban government to repudiate its early position and to aim to incorporate LGBT people into all facets of socialist construction.

A socialist revolution has yet to occur in an economically devel-oped country. Most took place in countries that still had semi-feudal social relations, particularly in the countryside. None had a mass LGBT movement before the revolution.

The United States, however, is a developed proletarian country. LGBT people are already visible and active as leaders and rank and file members in many aspects of the class struggle. In fact, the LGBT movement has served as a source of inspiration for many of the most militant activists of every movement. For example, the slogan, "Stand up! Fight back!" arose out of the AIDS struggles of the 1980s.

By overthrowing the capitalist class, the working class clears the road for a society where anti-LGBT oppression, like racism and sexism, will be a thing of the past. That is why LGBT activists and leaders fighting for dignified and equal lives are so deeply involved in the struggle for socialism. □

Socialist planning or capitalist profits

What can save the environment?

THE global environmental crisis is growing. Global warming as a result of human activity, shrinking polar caps, widespread pollution, growing shortages of basic resources like water—all these problems have been confirmed by international teams of scientists time and time again over the last three decades.

Global warming as a direct result of industrial pollution was confirmed by the United Nation's Intergovernmental Panel on Climate Change in a February 2007 report.[1] That body also confirmed the growing water shortages. The shrinking polar caps and rising ocean levels have been confirmed by both The National Snow and Ice Data Center and NASA Jet Propulsion Laboratories.

Workers and progressives all over the world are concerned about the rapidly deteriorating health of the environment. There is mounting anger against the multi-billion-dollar transnational corporations like Exxon-Mobil, Dow Chemical and Duke Energy—the main culprits in environmental destruction.

Millions of people volunteer time or give donations to environmental causes and organizations. According to a 2007 Harris poll, 77 percent of people in the United States recycle.

People all over the world, especially from oppressed countries, are fighting to stop the exploitation, destruction and pollution of their air, soil and water by the imperialist countries.

For example, in Cochabamba, Bolivia, a mass movement stopped the U.S. corporation Bechtel's attempt to privatize drinking water in 2000. Starting in 2002, a militant mass movement in Nigeria has confronted foreign oil companies like Chevron and Shell, shutting down plants and pipelines and winning many concessions like cleaner drilling and having oil wealth pay for schools and medical clinics.

The U.S. corporate media covers the environment on a regular basis. Al Gore and other imperialist politicians claim to champion the cause. Rock stars put on massive concerts to raise awareness and money to save the environment.

The United States is one of the main sources of pollution. It is also by far the wealthiest country in the world. Yet the U.S. government continues to do nothing to help stop this dangerous crisis. With the urgency of the problem for everyone, one would think that Washington would put its vast economic, scientific and technological resources into motion.

But that is not happening. Instead, working people are forced to pay billions of dollars for imperialist wars as funding for badly needed services is mercilessly slashed.

Why is there no well-funded worldwide task force to save the environment?

The impending danger to the planet is a very serious threat that all progressives and revolutionaries must analyze and struggle to reverse. The most basic question to resolve is: Can the environmental crisis be challenged within the framework of world capitalism?

THE INDUSTRIAL REVOLUTION

Capitalism emerged out of the restrictions of feudal Europe. In the course of revolutions in the Netherlands in the late 16th century, England in the late 17th century, France in 1789, political systems more adapted to the capitalist mode of production completely uprooted feudal economies based on large landed estates and the exploitation of peasant labor through serfdom.

As a system of production, capitalism is superior to the communal, slave and feudal economies that preceded it in terms of developing the productive forces of society. Surplus value, or profit, created through capitalist exploitation of labor has driven a rapid advance in production, science and technology.

Capitalist production gave a great impetus to the productive capabilities of society, beginning in the period of the Industrial Revolution in Europe in the 19th century and in the United States in the late 19th and early 20th centuries. Improved means of production under capitalism included the proliferation of machines; innovations in energy and the powering of machines using steam and coal; the harnessing of electricity; improved means of transportation by land (railway) and sea (steamship); the advent of factories; improved mining techniques; the development of a chemical industry; and a greater knowledge of metallurgy, which led to the production of iron and steel.

From 1800 to 1900, the productive capacity of the capitalist countries ballooned from 20 percent to 80 percent of the world's total production.[2] Giant industrial monopolies in steel, automobile, oil, agriculture, meat processing and many others became the most powerful institutions in such countries as England, France and the United States. By 1904, for example, Rockefeller's Standard Oil controlled 91 percent of U.S. oil production.

In those and other countries, this period saw a massive transformation of economic relations, ending up with industrial armies of workers on one side, and a tiny minority of wealthy owners, or capitalists, on the other side.

This was also the period that capitalism rapidly developed into monopoly capitalism, or imperialism, with a few corporations dominating whole industries and racing around the world to colonize, plunder and underdevelop whole continents. All this in a feverish pursuit to amass and concentrate the greatest wealth possible.

In Southern Africa, British imperialist Cecil Rhodes and his infamous mining company, De Beers, ruled the British colony of Rhodesia with the twin fists of plunder and racism. After a fierce liberation struggle, Rhodesia became the countries of Zambia and Zimbabwe.

Industrialization, with its ever-increasing need for natural resources and its intrinsic need to constantly revolutionize production, also brought with it extraordinary demands on the environment.

The face of the earth has gone through great changes in the last 250 years. Entire forests have been destroyed; many bays, rivers, lakes and streams have been contaminated with industrial and agricultural runoff; many species have been driven to extinction due to hunting and environmental changes; and entire mountain sides have been gutted in a relentless search for minerals.

Industrialization has meant that air pollution has been a constant threat. In 1873, the first in a series of killer smogs occurred in London. Over 1,150 people died in three days from severe air pollution from coal burning.

Workers now live in huge, sprawling cities. That is where the jobs are. Factories, refineries, power plants and cars located in these cities emit harmful toxins into the water, air and land. Oppressed communities, especially African-Americans, immigrants and Latinos, live in the most polluted neighborhoods.

According to a Congressional Black Caucus report, 70 percent of African Americans live in counties that violate federal air pollution standards. In every one of the 44 major metropolitan areas in the United States, African Americans are more likely than whites to be exposed to higher concentrations of toxins in the air they breathe.[3]

In underdeveloped countries and around the world, the environmental depredations of oil, mining, agricultural and chemical companies know no bounds.

One of the most infamous environmental accidents occurred in 1984 in Bhopal, India. A Union Carbide pesticide plant accident released dozens of toxic gases into the air. Some 8,000 people died in the first three days after the leak. In all, 20,000 people died as a result of the accident.

In the days following the disaster, Union Carbide lied and claimed that the leaked gases were really a potent tear gas. Refusal

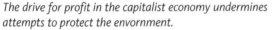

The drive for profit in the capitalist economy undermines attempts to protect the envornment.

PHOTO: CUSTOM MEDICAL STOCK PHOTO

of the company to disclose accurate information about the leak led to misdiagnoses and many unnecessary deaths.

Every year there are on average 20 to 40 major oil spills of anywhere from hundreds of tons to a million tons. Toxic oil spills cause immense damage to wildlife and have dire effects on water quality. Crude oil is made up of harmful chemicals like benzene, toluene and polycyclic aromatic hydrocarbons.

One of the largest recent oil spills happened in Lebanon in 2006 when Israeli jets bombed the Jiyeh Power Station during the U.S.-backed Israeli war on Lebanon. That attack released 30,000 tons of oil into the Mediterranean. The biggest oil spill in history happened as a result of the U.S. war against Iraq in 1991. Over 1 million tons of oil were spilled into the Persian Gulf. At the beginning of the war, U.S. planes bombed oil tankers, pipelines and holding tanks.[4]

A January 2004 Friends of the Earth study estimated that one company alone—the U.S. oil giant Exxon Mobil—has contributed 5 percent of the world's total carbon dioxide emissions over the 120-year period from 1882 to 2002.[5] Carbon dioxide is one of the "greenhouse gases" that is linked to global warming.

U.S. IMPERIALISM OPPOSES PROGRESS

Preventing further environmental ruin is not a priority for the U.S. government or its masters in the capitalist class.

A 2006 study by scientists from Britain's most prestigious professional science academy, the Royal Society, revealed that the United States emitted more greenhouse gases in 2004 than at any time in history. "Total U.S. emissions have risen by 15.8 percent between 1990 and 2004, mainly due to increased consumption of electricity generated by the burning of fossil fuel, a rise in energy demands caused by increased industrial production, and a rise in petrol consumption due to increased travel."[6]

The U.S. capitalist class, however, will not agree to cut emissions by even the smallest amount. The Bush administration, like the Clinton administration before, refuses to submit the extremely weak protocols of the Kyoto treaty on global warming to the U.S. Senate for ratification. The Kyoto protocols aim to reduce world emissions by only 5.2 percent by 2012.

Despite his rather weak record as vice president from 1992 to 2000, Al Gore has emerged as the most visible "pro-environment" capitalist politician in the U.S. ruling-class circles. Gore's environmental film, "An Inconvenient Truth," has increased public knowledge of the scientific consensus on the causes of global warming through carbon emissions. But Gore's solution to the problem of global warming is based on misleading programs like carbon trading and biofuels.

Carbon trading is a market-oriented system as opposed to a rational plan to stop global warming. Polluting companies would get credits to emit a certain amount of carbon. If a company does not emit as much carbon as it is allowed, that company can sell its left over carbon emissions credit to another company, which can then emit more.

Gore has also been a proponent of biofuels, which are heavily promoted on the website of his foundation, the Alliance for Climate Protection. Most biofuels are currently made from food crops such as corn, resulting in an increase in prices for corn, milk and other foods. For countries where corn is a staple, like Mexico, the increase in corn prices has hurt working-class people. A greater emphasis on biofuels is destined to lead to artificial and real food shortages as the price of corn rises with increased demand.

SOCIALIST REVOLUTION AND THE ENVIRONMENT

In the same way capitalist production overcame the feudal relations of handicraft and landed estates, socialist production offers the possibility of releasing workers and oppressed people from the chains of capitalist relations.

To this point in history, workers have taken power and set out to construct socialist societies within the bounds of countries whose economies had not gone through full capitalist development prior to the revolution. While the relative weakness of the capitalist and ruling classes in countries like Russia and China made revolutions more possible, the task of socialist economic planning and construction is made much more difficult within the confines of a less-developed economy.

Socialism as a mode of production that seeks to meet the needs of the entire society relies on the complete industrialization of society and the fully developed working class that goes along with it. Because they must develop their economies or be overturned and brought back into the imperialist orbit, independent countries like China, Iran, Venezuela, Cuba and others have to make difficult choices.

The primary concern of any oppressed country, whether or not they have had a socialist, national or anti-colonial revolution, is the development of the means of production. Revolutionaries and progressives defend all oppressed nations' rights to develop their economies on their own terms as an essential component in their struggle against the predations of U.S. and other imperialist powers.

IS CHINA THE REAL PROBLEM?

Listening to the U.S. ruling class media today, any worker would think that the main environmental problem in the world today is China. Beginning in August 2007, for example, the New York Times ran a series of articles called "Choking on growth: China's environmental crisis." The September/October 2007 issue of Foreign Affairs, an influential ruling-class journal, ran an article called "The great leap backwards," which argued, "China is fast becoming one of the leading industrial polluters in the world." The Council on Foreign Relations devoted an extensive report in February 2007 to "China's environmental crisis."

The 1949 socialist revolution in China took place in a vast country where poverty, starvation, drought and misery were routine for hundreds of millions of people. Colonial bondage at the hands of Japanese, British, French, German and U.S. imperialists had left the country incapable of providing for the basic needs of its people.

China's much-needed and rapid development has come with consequences. The country is plagued by the same environmental problems that imperialist countries faced during their industrialization. Seventy percent of China's energy production comes from burning coal—42 percent higher than the world's average. Many of China's cities suffer from excessive air pollution and smog as a result.

China does face a pollution crisis. It has contributed to the broader global problem of global warming and environmental crisis. But China's situation as a country emerging from colonial exploitation cannot be compared to a developed country like the United States.

On the one hand, much of China's pollution is due in large part to the colonial legacy of underdevelopment and foreign ownership of industrial companies that export goods primarily to imperialist countries.

On the other hand, China's retention of some central planning gives them tools to combat corporate criminals that workers in imperialist countries do not have. For example, the Chinese government's 11th Five-Year Plan aims at reducing energy consumption by 20 percent, while the discharge of sulfur dioxide and other pollutants should drop by 10 percent.[7]

Also in 2007, China unveiled two important strategic plans for sustainable development: the Action Plan on Environment and Health and the National Climate Change Program. The former is designed "to guide environmental and health work in a scientific way," according to a Jan. 5 posting on China.org.cn. "Positive public health is mandatory for sustainable social and economic development," the report notes.

The National Climate Change Program commits the Chinese government to "swiftly adopt measures ranging from laws, economy, administration and technology which will combine to reduce greenhouse gas emissions and imbue the country with a flexible approach to climate change."[8]

SOCIALIST CUBA

Cuba is the world's leader in developing a sustainable, environmentally responsible economy.

Socialist economies are based on central planning, a tool which offers the key to resolving the contradictions between national development, human well-being and care for the environment.

Cuba's environmental revolution has happened at a time when the island's economic development is still far behind countries like the United States, Britain and France. In part, Cuba has turned toward large-scale programs like organic agriculture out of necessity. The overthrow of the Soviet Union and Eastern European socialist countries meant that Cuba had to look for ways to greatly increase food production without imported fertilizer and pesticides and without their main trading partners. In 1990 and 1991 alone, Cuba lost 80 percent of its foreign trade.

Central planning during the "special period" that followed the collapse of the Soviet Union was essential for the survival of the Cuban Revolution. Public ownership of the means of production made the switch to sustainable production much easier.

According to the World Wildlife Foundation's 2006 "Living Planet Report," Cuba is the only country in the world to meet the standards for sustainability using two indices—the World Wildlife Federation's ecological footprint measure and the United Nations Development Program's Human Development Index. The HDI is calculated based on life expectancy, literacy and per capita gross domestic product. An HDI value greater than 0.8 is considered to be "high human development."

The ecological footprint measures "demand on the biosphere in terms of the area of biologically productive land and sea required" to provide resources and absorb waste. A nation's footprint includes, "cropland, grazing land, forest and fishing grounds required to produce the food, fiber and timber it consumes," to absorb the waste produced and to provide space for infrastructure.[9]

The footprint is measured in terms of "global hectares" per person per country. The global average footprint is 1.8 hectares, so a footprint size lower than 1.8 denotes sustainable use. The United States' footprint is 9.5 hectares. Only Cuba had an HDI value of 0.8 or greater combined with an ecological footprint of 1.8 or lower.

With socialist planning and distribution, environmentally sound production is attainable. Socialist production on the basis of human needs eliminates the incentive to waste resources in pursuit of short-term profit present under capitalism. Under socialism, there is greater incentive to plan for sustainable development, stewarding natural resources for future generations.

WHO WILL SAVE THE ENVIRONMENT?

The criminal capitalist class is unsuited to lead a movement to save the environment. It is in their nature to oppose anything that diminishes their ability to profit from exploiting the earth, its people, and every other thing on the planet.

Struggle and organizing can bring about change in environmental standards and regulations. It has in the past.

A 1970s California grassroots movement to reduce smog led to stricter regulations and cleaner skies. A 2007 grassroots campaign in Indiana and Illinois stopped British Petroleum from increasing their heavy metal dumping into Lake Michigan. Renewed struggles in this vein are very much needed now.

But the capitalist system does not produce rational strategies or outcomes. Competition between enterprises prevents the kind of national, much less international, economic planning that can both provide for peoples needs and do it in a manner that puts a premium on ecological sustainability. Each corporate CEO, no matter what they feel and think about the environment, makes decisions with one goal in mind: to maximize profit each quarter for the investor class. If they make a decision that is good for the environment but bad for profits, they will be quickly fired.

Only a global system based on economic planning instead of on cutthroat competition can offer the framework for making decisions that favor the environmental needs of the entire planet rather than satisfy the narrow needs of investors seeking the biggest return. This is an essential difference between a world capitalist economy and a world socialist economy.

Capitalism revolutionized the means of production over the past five centuries. Industrial and scientific development, operating together under the impetus of national and now international competition for the world market, created the material basis for eliminating hunger and want.

It also created an unplanned assault on the core ecosystems of the planet.

People will never go back to the pre-bourgeois period, the stage of society that pre-dates industrialization. Industrial society is a reality that offers great promise toward eliminating poverty and want.

Now, though, the collective property that has welded the people of all continents together as a world economy must be liberated from capitalist ownership and converted to public property. That alone offers the hope and possibility for an economic development plan based on international planning that both meets human needs and protects and restores the health of the global environment.

Communism offers society the way back from the precipice. □

Endnotes

1. "Science panel calls global warming 'unequivocal'," New York Times, Feb. 3, 2007.
2. Paul Bairoch, "International Industrialization Levels from 1750 to 1980," Journal of European Economic History Vol. 11, No. 2 (Fall 1982), p. 269-325.

3. Kenya Covington "Climate change and extreme weather events: An unequal burden on African Americans," Congressional Black Caucus Foundation Inc., Center for Policy Analysis and Research Report, No. 2, September 2005.

4. Friedhelm Krupp and Peter Symens, "Gulf Sanctuary," Arabian Wildlife Vol. 1, No. 1, January 1994, http://www.arabianwildlife. com/archive/vol1.1/sanct.htm.

5. "Exxon's climate footprint," Friends of the Earth International, London, 2004, http://www.foe.org/camps/intl/exxons_climate_footprint.pdf.

6. The Independent, April 19, 2006.

7. Xinhua News, March 8, 2007.

8. China.org.cn, June 4, 2007, china.org.cn/english/environment /213624.htm.

9. World Wildlife Fund, Living Planet Report 2006, http://assets. panda.org/downloads/living_planet_report.pdf, p. 16.

LiberationNews.org
Website of the Party for Socialism and Liberation

HOME   ABOUT   BLOGGERS   ARCHIVES   PUBLICATIONS   JOIN THE PSL   CONTACT US   DONATE

Featuring
• News
• Analysis
• Militant Journalism
• Video and Podcasts
• Downloadable Posters and Art
• Event Listings and more!

Made in the USA
Monee, IL
29 December 2020